For our Life is but a Song

For our
Life
is but a
Song

Memories of Damian Lundy

Benet Conroy FSC
and Gerard Rummery FSC

McCrimmons
Great Wakering, Essex, England

First published in the United Kingdom in 2000 by
McCRIMMON PUBLISHING CO. LTD.
10-12 High Street, Great Wakering, Essex, England
Telephone 01702-218956   Fax 01702-216082
Email: mccrimmons@dial.pipex.com
Website: www.mccrimmons.co.uk

© 2000 Benet Conroy FSC and Gerard Rummery FSC

Edited by Paul Davis

ISBN 0 85597 624 1

British Library Cataloguing in Publication Data.
A catalogue record for this book is available from the British Library.

Cover design and layout by Nick Snode
Typeset in Revival (Berling) 11 and 10pt roman
Printed and bound in England by Thanet Press Ltd., Margate, Kent   G/00

Contents

Acknowledgements

We wish to express our thanks to so many people that it would take a book to mention you all. A great many of Damian's friends are present in this book, some in a major incident or a poem or a story, others in a nuance or a phrase. You contribute to a vibrant tapestry, the whole made up of many threads. Some of you are named, but others are anonymous or incognito. There are, as the writer of the Letter to the Hebrews acknowledges, "so many witnesses in a cloud all around us" and the cloud drops its rain and waters a sentence, an event, an insight. Your gift to this book is that you touched Damian's life and so ours in the writing. Hundreds of you wrote after his death and many have been kind and allowed us to use extracts from letters and appreciations. Please accept our gratitude, all of you who make up Damian's extended family.

We are grateful for particular help:

Brothers Dominic Green and Joseph Hendron
    (St Cassian's foundation).
Brother Nicholas Hutchinson
    (Ninian Park and Lasallian Resource).
Mrs Vi Lundy
    (family history and events).
Sr Luala and Sr Petronilla
    (Damian's family and childhood).
Fr Jim Gallagher and Sr Bernadette
    (the National Project, for verses, fun and a fund of stories).

Anne White
(resources, insights and encouragement).
The Dowle family
(the Malt House poem and letter, and Kintbury).
Vin and Bernie Kilty and Aidan Kilty
(music and song and stories).
Sr Dorothy Costigan
(letters and the poem addressed to her).
Bishop David Konstant
(homily at the Kensington Mass).
Sr Louisa Poole
(*To Live is to Change*, and photographs)
Sr Maeve McDevitt
(the Key Catechists programme).
Dom Edmund Flood and Dom Christopher Jamison
(catechetics and writings).
Brother Damian Roe
(Oxford Archives of the De La Salle Brothers).
To *The Tablet* and *Priests and People*
(articles published by or about Damian).
Gerry Markland
(songs and poems)
Marie-Clair Goswell
(who proof-read over and over again)
Shona and David Tildesley for permission to include the
poem 'For Alistair'.

We thank those who have kindly given permission for use of copyright materials. Every effort has been made to trace the copyright holders but if any has been inadvertently overlooked, the authors and publishers will be pleased to make the necessary arrangement at the first opportunity.

Brother Benet Conroy
Brother Gerard Rummery

Introduction

From the funeral eulogy given by:
Brother Joseph Hendron, Provincial,
De La Salle Brothers, Great Britain, 1996–2000

I had the privilege of spending two lengthy periods with Damian in Community in the 1960s and 1970s when he was in good health and his energy and enthusiasm were at their peak. It was the period just after the Second Vatican Council, a time of great promise, but also a time of trauma for some, and not least for Religious Orders. The documents of Vatican II were coming on stream. Those on Liturgical renewal were of particular interest to Damian, since he saw Liturgy as a key element in all worthwhile renewal. Without delay he set about implementing them. This was no mere rearranging of furniture; primarily it was aimed at people – at helping people live the new insights. Personally I owe a lot to him for interpreting the new directions and putting them into practice; it was an exciting time. I confess that there were times when I worried and wondered *'Will this or that new approach work? Has he gone too far?'* But always it *did* work, and I felt afterwards *'now I see things differently'*. He was no iconoclast; he had a deep appreciation and reverence for the sacred, for all that Liturgy meant. When some objected that everything from the past was being discarded and thrown out, even such simple things as candles and charcoal and incense and holy water, he would reply "No, these will continue to be used. They are necessary and effective signs and symbols" and as anyone who has participated with him in Liturgy will know, he could gather in everything from leaves and stones to personal belongings and the banal artistic and literary efforts of children or adults, and use them for worship. They were the gifts of people and must be respected and included in prayer or worship. People sprinkled with Holy water should feel that they are being sprinkled – bring an umbrella if you feel at risk! Offer each one a lighted candle and give him/her the time to encounter in it the light and life of Christ.

Inevitably his work and influence, and his public profile, attracted a measure of criticism and hostility. Damian was a man of dialogue, who loved to converse, hear the other's point of view, and respond with his own, but without antagonism or acrimony. To be condemned without a hearing, for one who was himself a wonderful listener, left him mystified rather than angry. Difficulties are there to be discussed and talked through, not piled up in evidence against people. Let us look at them together. He bore no grudges; he might find criticism painful but in his dealings with people he was always gracious and caring.

Those who only knew him through *Songs of the Spirit* or his writings or his talks, were not always aware of his other gifts. He was a talented stage actor, and loved the theatre. To go with him to the theatre was almost like being on the stage itself. He would enter into the drama as though he were one of the cast. His school productions were famous for their originality and professionalism. Some of the most memorable talks I heard him give were on English Literature, scholarly lectures sprinkled with humorous digressions and anecdotes.

But it is as a Brother in Religious Life that I knew Damian best. As I said, I had the privilege of spending two lengthy periods with him in Community in the 1960s and 1970s. I cannot remember when I first met him – and this in itself is significant. On a first meeting there would be nothing remarkable about him, no show of learning or pretence or self-importance and attention-seeking. One grew to appreciate him by being with him. He was a delightful companion. In addition to the gifts already alluded to, he was an excellent chef. In fact he had signed up already to cook the Christmas dinner for the Community this year. Whoever takes over this task now will have to reach a high standard. He loved cooking, but not shopping. "Get me the items from the shop or supermarket and I will enjoy doing the rest," he said recently. "I dislike shopping." But cooking also enabled him to serve his brothers; it would be difficult to decide which was more important to him, the cooking or the service. Service was central in all his relationships. In all the time that I lived with him I never knew him to cook just for himself. If there was anyone else in the house he would always, always invite them to join him, saying something like: "can I do you something, would you have a bit of this? I'm cooking; why not try a bit of this?" He liked his food when he was in full health. I am sure he will be delighted to get back now to enjoying Isaiah's banquet mentioned in the first reading.

The   *'feast of rich **food**, a feast of well-aged wines,*
          *of rich food filled with **marrow**,*
          of well-aged wines strained clear.'

Come 10.30 or 11.00 at night when people were thinking of moving off to bed I can still see the community room door opening and there was Damian, in one hand a huge tray of sandwiches and in the other two large jugs spilling beer, and a greeting: "Cheers, would anyone like a little sandwich before we retire?" and then you knew you were there for another hour at least, because Damian's few minutes ended up as hours. Groups at Conferences would be told: 'We will finish in exactly half an hour'; but they never did. He did not drive and times for departure or arrival were always approximate, partly because no one could just be turned away from, because of a deadline. His or her story or worry or question had to be heard and dealt with. The healing was in the respect and listening. To come back to the beer and sandwiches. These provided the occasion for a review of the day; and often, and imperceptibly, each one present would be affirmed by Damian by some seemingly chance remark about how he

(Damian) had appreciated or liked what each had said or done that day, whether it was that the lawn had been cut or a good talk had been given.

As a community and as a Province, we will miss him for what he was to us as a person more than for his writings and cooking and singing and the many other gifts that he generously shared. We would have liked to have him with us in good health for many more years, but even in sickness and suffering he was an inspiration and a tower of strength. We mourn his death but thank God for all his relatively short life has meant to us and the Church.

1 | Gathered for a Thanksgiving Service

Our Lady of Victories, Kensington, was the place to be on 2nd July 1997, for this was a memorial Mass for Damian jointly arranged by The Bishops' Conference Religious Education Department, the National Project Team and the National Board of Religious Inspectors and Advisors. Martin Foster of the Liturgy Office arranged the service and the creative, lively and moving music. It felt as if everyone Damian had touched in life was there to make sure he was celebrated fittingly. The murmuring flood gathered and eventually burst into song, inspired by Damian's music, lyrics, his indomitable approach, and accompanied by much skill, talent and verve.

The celebration offered a bird's-eye view of his life and achievements, a tableau of his many talents and gifts, and it was Bishop Konstant's homily that provided the resumé that all could easily handle: Damian like a conductor with a scratch orchestra; the teacher, pastor or shepherd; writer of hymns, scholar and student, catechist; teacher of prayer, a reconciler; Damian the De La Salle Brother. Damian was such a rich character that occasional meetings with him revealed a little something, but there were facets that only came to the fore after multiple visits to the well that was Damian.

What drew people to Kensington? Perhaps it was Damian's ability to affirm, to bring the best out of people. To make a dawn chorus of unlikely songbirds. Was it an early experience he had that proved prophetic – for him and others? An experience that touched him personally and convinced him of the importance of affirmation? And in Lasallian terms, an apparently insignificant meeting took on global proportions?

The circumstances are vague but the story simple and powerful. One day Damian (a young teenager) met an elderly man and they got chatting. Curiosity (which got the better of Simeon) is such a rich virtue.

"Where are you from?".

"Halifax".

"Which part?"

"Actually I'm from Sowerby Bridge."

"Never forget, lad, that Sowerby Bridge is a Constituency in its own right!"

Can anything good come from Nazareth? It can, and from Sowerby Bridge, and anywhere else! Part of Damian's life from then on was naturally and spontaneously devoted to helping each one he met to discover the thrill of being affirmed. Thanks, old man, for your insight; God works in marvellous ways and you were a prophetic chance meeting.

God's wonderful ways revealed in Damian were very much the subject of Bishop Konstant's homily. He began with that first glimpse of Damian which many had, of the welcome party at Kintbury.

"My first memory of Damian is at Kintbury, that large, comfortable figure, completely at ease – guiding young people to discover, understand, be glad about, celebrate their faith, and to begin to realise that their faith – inchoate, inarticulate, unformed – was part of the faith of the Church.

Like a conductor with a scratch orchestra, he discovered new instruments, giving players confidence to try them out and to learn what they were capable of. The concert was always fresh, never polished, always worthwhile because, though rough music, it was genuine, true, creative, imaginative and hopeful. I was struck both by his quite remarkable gifts and by his lovely simplicity and humility and, of course, his gifts from God.

Damian was a gifted spirit, who used (and was encouraged to use) his gifts to the full. As a De La Salle Brother for more than thirty-five years he was a teacher (in secondary school), a pastor or shepherd (especially at Kintbury), a writer (of hymns, and for the National Project), scholar or student (witnessed by his recent PhD from Manchester, and his involvement in Adult Catechesis).

The reading from Ephesians was so well chosen: "I pray with joy for your partnership in the gospel" for Damian's work was simply, solely and powerfully for the gospel. He was an evangelist in all he did; he made the gospel real for others and brought people to Christ and to the Church. He bore much fruit and was a true disciple of Christ, and this, as we heard in the gospel for today, is to the Father's glory.

His memorial will be first of all those with whom he shared his faith, led to faith, encouraged in faith and taught to pray – many of whom are doubtless present this evening. I suspect we shall be surprised to discover, when we see God, those to whom we have shown some image of God. Damian will be no less surprised than any of us. The first fruits of his life and death, therefore, are people – men and women of all ages. They are praying in gratitude for him, some by being here, others as they call him to mind: "Let all the fruits that we have borne, be for him an assurance of joy and salvation". Whatever his faults may have been, his love is weightier: "Above all hold unfailing your love for one another, since love covers a multitude of sins" (1 Peter 4:8).

A second memorial is in what he wrote, not primarily his catechetical writings, valuable though these are, but in his hymns. I hope he would forgive me if I say these are not all great literature; most of them were written (I imagine) in response to the needs of particular groups at Kintbury, but they do show some of his priorities. In remembering him we can reflect on these, as guidance for our own growth.

A recurring theme is reconciliation, that healing brought by the crucified Christ:

Soon a man will come with arms outstretched
at the rising of the sun,
His wounded hands will set you free
if you take these for your own.

Jesus is Lord!
Be still for he
will come with healing, quietly.
Deep in your heart, you'll hear his voice,
and in the stillness you'll rejoice.

The image of Christ's outstretched arms is frequent:

His arm outstretched to protect you in danger
he never sleeps, all the time he is watching.
He is the maker of the skies,
but he knows your name, he hears your cries.
His loving care shelters you like a shadow,
to keep you safe from the evil around you.

Damian was so conscious of the fears of many young people: fears of isolation, of being ignored, of inadequacy, of the unknown, and he wanted to reassure them of Christ's loving presence:

Christ, your Son, is always near,
so we journey without fear
singing as we walk along:
Christ our joy, and Christ our song!

People everywhere ask for healing, forgiveness, reassurance and these can only be given by the risen Lord:

He is the Lord who conquers death…
The Christ who died is Lord of life…
We are healed – he has bound our wounds…
He calls us together as one…

There is a marked progression in many of his songs: reconciliation, healing, freedom, unity, suffering, death, resurrection, glory – and this is the progression of the gospel.

Unless a grain of wheat dies, it remains a single grain, but if it dies it bears much fruit.

Therein, of course, lay the ultimate gift Damian was asked to accept, the gift of suffering that he knew would lead to dying. A cross indeed, but a gift too. Was he thinking of this when he wrote:

If death's anguish fills my mind
with dismay and trembling,
in my night I call on you, Lord,
and you give me strength.

In this I am reminded of Hebrews: 'Any discipline is at the time a matter for grief, not joy; but later, in those who have undergone it, it bears fruit in peace and uprightness. So steady all weary hands and trembling knees' and elsewhere, 'my grace is sufficient for you'.

The discipline of sickness brought its own fruits: he was happy, contented, did what his strength let him do. That it was an anguish indeed, a pathway to God, none can doubt. In that hymn of praise he wrote, based on Francis of Assisi's own paean of praise and joy, he spoke of:

those who share your peace with others,
bearing trials and sickness bravely.
Even sister death won't harm them.

As we pray in the introduction to the Eucharistic Prayer, 'his life is changed, not ended'. We pray for him, that, as Paul prayed for the Ephesians, his 'love may grow complete'. We pray that we and many others may benefit from the fruits of a life so generously, faithfully and happily lived for Jesus Christ, and for so many of his friends."

Eternal rest give unto him O Lord,
and let perpetual light shine upon him.
May he rest in peace. Amen.

This celebration tribute hopes to give a taste (with zest) of the vital, profound, humorous, fun-loving, deep, intellectual, humble, spiritual, suffering, prayerful, cultured, well travelled, musical, dramatic, poetic and occasionally controversial Damian. It offers those who visit it a chance to relive their experience of the man: hands-on, tinglingly exciting, devastatingly simple and shudderingly profound almost twenty-four hours a day. Visit and relive, visit and discover! Here is a treasure house whose owner brought out new things and old, and who enabled visitors to discover their own treasure house.

Nelson Mandela, in his inaugural speech, encouraged all to recognise their gifts and to reveal them, for in so doing others are liberated to develop their gifts. Damian had this effect: he liberated, he inaugurated a process of discovery. And it did not matter who you were, for Damian was all things to all. There is a story about a conductor who was invited to direct a minor orchestra. During one of the more successful sessions he turned to his first violin and whispered, not so *sotto voce:* "Don't look now, but I think we're being followed!" This touch of mischief, the glint in the eye, the delight in others' success, the thrill of having enabled and then stood back to watch the virtuoso performance of a so-called minor orchestra, were part of the experience of Damian. His was a biblical vision which saw God's hand in every aspect of life, saw how God worked and was inspired to follow the example God gave. Damian discovered lots of Ruths, collecting the scattered gleanings; tuned in to many a reluctant prophet timid of voice; met oceans of young people hungry for life-giving food and dying of thirst. This was probably why his description of St. Cassian's, Kintbury, was of a well, for the article he wrote for the 1996 jubilee was "A Journey to the Inner Place"; typically, his conclusion to the visit to the well is "The more you give away, the more you have and the thirstier you become".

I wonder if Damian's dad's skill as a Master Baker had anything to do with Damian's way of operating: take simple ingredients, mix, add some inspiration and provide heat! He loved listening to the Crafty Cook on Classic FM at 10.30 each morning, whether in the office or in the car. Food fascinated Damian; his life was spent trying to offer it to others. As Bucky Fuller would say, "we are designed to be constantly re-hungered, re-thirsted and multiplyingly curious". It's a pity they never met.

But we did meet Damian. And how fortunate we were! Meeting him was often a challenge, but it was never a threat. Think? You had little choice. Respond? Yes, to an invitation. God calls, we listen; God invites, we respond; God saves, we change. This was one of his mantras. Go to a lecture or a session or a conference and he would offer a series of challenging questions, offer some guidelines, ask you to take time to think, to join others in a personal reflection, then come to a conclusion. If God calls, do I listen? Whatever the personal conclusion, it was always a challenge. When he responded to staff invitations for INSET, he tried to encourage positive thinking, largely by asking questions. Time and again he would provoke reaction: What do you do that is life-giving for others? What do you do that is not life-giving? He loved ecological scenarios. I suppose he had a good example in the teller of Sower parables.

But he also recognised his own limitations and was happy therefore to be eclectic – if this works I'll try it out! In one of his favourite books, *Collected Poems of W.B. Yeats*, he has a hand-written, insightful note in the margin: "Art's power. Art's limitations". The poem is *The Municipal Gallery Revisited*. Even here he recognised the gap that exists between a vision and its coming to reality. How often the cry "Mind the Gap!" rallied distracted thoughts or disparate groups. Time to focus! A journey on the Underground became a spiritual experience.

Damian's personal experience often brought him to clear conclusions, for one of his favourite scenes in *Shadowlands* is C. S. Lewis with his son, sharing for the first time their grief at the loss of Joy. The words come out strong, poignant: "Experience, you're a hard teacher. But, by God, we learn!" Damian's work nationally brought difficult, painful and threatening experiences. His contribution to the CES Directory was offered accompanied by the following letter to Fr. Faley:

> Here is my complete text. It has been written during a difficult time of ill health, pressures of commitments and responsibilities… I'll spare you the details! Do with it what you will. Feel completely free to adapt, add, change, etc. My name will not be on the end of it, and I wave farewell to the baby as I deposit it in your arms. I don't know if it is what the Bishops are looking for, but it is what I (and many teachers I know) would like them to say! Certainly it is intended to complement the excellent material prepared by Anne, Anthony and yourself (though neither section will placate the vociferous critics). The tone of my piece is reasonable, mild, but not, I hope,

sycophantic. Parts of it are uncompromising, and say a few things that I personally regard as relevant to the present rather heated debate which has been so disturbingly fuelled by recent articles and letters in the Catholic press. You will judge whether it is appropriate, and if you decide it is, it will be up to the Department to accept or to reject it. 'Here I stand. I can do no other.' (Am I wise to quote Martin Luther?)

Part of his contribution says this:

Catechesis is one of the Church's central ministries, since it seeks to make the word of God present as a living reality in the Christian community of today. It has never been an easy ministry to exercise, since it makes enormous demands on the faith, hope, charity, unity and vitality of the Catholic community as a whole, and since it is notoriously subject to misunderstandings and controversies.

The Church's mission to evangelise and to catechise the young must be distinguished from the religious education which is part of the curriculum in every school, though religious education given to children and young people in Catholic schools must always include sound instruction to educate and deepen their faith. Modern attempts to describe or define faith sometimes distinguish between the beliefs professed by Christians in the Creed, the relationship of trusting faith between God and believers, and the faith which motivates the attitudes and actions of believers. Moreover, contemporary Catholic pastoral theology emphasises that faith, while always a personal response to God's revelation, is never to be regarded as simply the response of an individual believer but as that person's participation in the life of the community of faith.

These are powerful comments, coming as they do from a leading international practitioner in the classroom, retreat centre, conference hall, parish and catechetical centre. He had the joy of instigating powerful renewal and his skills as compiler and song writer gave access to hearts he would not otherwise have had. His talent as an author took him to resource materials not easily accessible to all and helped him to develop his holistic view of evangelisation. But the pain is to be found there too. His insights come, like C.S. Lewis's, from that hard experience. His doctoral thesis focused especially on adult catechesis since Vatican II, for he was convinced that the Church would be wise to invest resources and personnel in the deepening of the faith of the parents not just the children. He has the ability to see the global picture, but he shows particular sensitivity and concern to those whom he recognises the Church has a special affection for:

> In the context of today, it is not surprising that our Catholic schools cater at once for children from very traditional Catholic families; children from very liberal Catholic families; children from single-parent families, who are often struggling to make ends meet; children from unevangelised, unchurched homes, which are nominally Catholic; Christian children who are not Catholics; children from other faiths; indeed some children without any specific religious background. Some Catholics regard this as a cause for anxiety, but let us recall that the Council itself asked Catholics 'to show special concern for the needs of those who are poor in the goods of this world or who are deprived of the assistance and affection of a family or who are strangers to the gift of faith' *(Declaration on Christian Education 9)*. Catholic schools welcome all these children, and seek to evangelise them by offering them a Christian education.

His sensitivity often comes from experience but also because he has been evangelised by those supposedly poor and by his deep personal reading of Church teaching. He frequently astonished his listeners by giving them insights into how the Church was responding to the poor, not least those who were "strangers to the gift of faith". It is a further example of his inclusiveness, and of a life lived according to Gospel values. He had an eye for history, the needs of today and for the millennium:

> As Cardinal Hume remarked in May 1996, in an address particularly relevant to Christian educators and their critics, patience and charity are of the greatest importance; 'Proclaiming the truth, not only in word but also in the way we act, is generally more successful than the outright condemnation of error.' These words echo the famous address of Pope John XXIII to the opening session of Vatican II. Since 'errors often vanish as swiftly as they arise, like mist before the sun', said the Pope, the Church

today prefers 'to use the medicine of mercy rather than severity. She considers that she meets the needs of the present age by showing the validity of her teaching rather than by condemnations'. Pope John told the Council fathers, 'Our task is not merely to hoard this precious treasure, as though obsessed with the past, but to give ourselves eagerly and without fear to the task that the present age demands of us – and in so doing we will be faithful to what the Church has done in the last twenty centuries.'

If a parable is a challenge, so was meeting Damian. At the back of Our Lady of Victories Church were large flip chart sheets and markers, each accompanied by an invitation from Anne White to write a tribute to Damian, free, spontaneous, celebratory. His personal impact came to life in the tributes.

What do these say? How do you respond to them, the briefest glimpses into revealing souls? How to encapsulate in a parcel of words a life changing meeting? Taste and see!

═══════════════════════

I hope I can sing your songs to the end of my life.

Mind the gap!

For unity of Spirit which passed all boundaries
– thanks be to God – may that continue.

Thanks Damian for the laughter.

The young of all ages will always carry your love and
joy of the Lord with them.

Thank you Damian for always being inclusive.

Courage and loving kindness.

Thank you Damian for teaching me how to pray.
Your book To Grow in Christ changed my life.

Thanks for your wonderful sharing of your gift of song to make Him known.

Thank you for deepening and awakening faith.
Thank you for showing me how to be humble.

Damian, you started it all for me – thank you.

I hope you would be happy to see the person I've become
– with your help. XX

Laudato Sii for Damian. YES! YES!

For unity of Spirit which passed all boundaries – thanks be to God – may that continue.

Bury the hatchet. Don't mark the spot!

A Yorkshire man in whom there was no guile!

You often said "God does not make junk. He collects it!"
Thanks for helping the junk.
Thank you for uplifting times.

One of the best books on prayer: To Grow in Christ.

For all the profound positive influences on youth work in this country:
residentials; catechetics; liturgy;
keeping things accessible and fun;
without losing the plot.

Now then people... time for inner sustenance... Grub!

The Singer and the Song of Christ.

Thank you Damian for being our life is but a song –
celebration.
And for your joy.

Suffering Jesus to the rescue.

Damian said "Jesus calls and it behoves us to respond".

Do it today!
Thank you for all your wonderful music
and for being such a marvellous and inspiring person.

For your music, sense of humour in certain circumstances –
"getting" 400 people to open their mouths and sing
– and enjoy it!
THANK YOU above all keeping Jesus central for us.
Deo gratias! Alleluia!

Cheerful, funny, always complaining of having to sit up
on his portable machine at 2 in the morning.

Say "Yes!" and "Yippee!"

Join the dance of all creation.

Added to these could be the hundreds of tributes which poured in after his death, each one bearing witness to how Damian had touched lives. He showed how God is a personal friend; spiritual things daily bread; he enabled the uncertain to turn vague longings into realised dreams; he set hearts singing which before were tone-deaf. And he was as likely to do this over a sandwich, a spontaneous song, a chat with a pint, a joke, or a rattling good story. He seemed indefatigable; yet in a way he was destined to fulfil through dramatic irony, some of his own insights and prophecies. How many songs of his deal with pain and suffering? Well before his heart and kidney problems he wrote his Easter hymn (quoted by Bishop Konstant):

> Soon a man will come with arms outstretched
> at the rising of the sun.
> His wounded hands will set you free
> if you take these for your own.

Damian took these hands and became a healer; he took the hands of the young, recognising their loneliness, their fear, their uncertainty, and he led them to Christ our joy, Christ our song. Damian took the hands of the whole family and similar to Jesus' closing words to Peter: "Shall we walk on together?" He was prepared to share the anguish and the pain, the joy and the creativity. He recognised the incredible generosity of God and became a reconciler. Paul would have been delighted with him!

All this is from God, who reconciled us to himself through Christ, and has given us the ministry of reconciliation.
[2 Cor 5:18]

Read on. Relive your own experience of the man with whom we were gifted for but fifty-two years. Then go out and be good news.

2 | The life of Damian (Michael) Lundy

This chapter will give a quick overview of Damian's life, a précis-biography which can be expanded by reference to other chapters in the book.

Prior to the Second Vatican Council, it was usual when someone joined a religious order that there would be a change of name. There was good scriptural precedent for this – Abram becoming Abraham, Sarai becoming Sara, Simon becoming Peter, Saul becoming Paul. And so Michael became Damian. The arrangement often caused amusement, especially as family still used the Baptismal name, and friends phoning up often asked for the person by the name they had known them by for years! Especially as it was unusual to use a surname. This is a simple preliminary for the exchange of names that takes place in this chapter!

Michael (I mean Damian-to-be) was born on March 21st 1944 in the small town of Sowerby Bridge, Yorkshire (hence the Yorkshireman in whom was no guile). His mum was Mary and his dad was James. His younger brother, Terence, was born in 1946. Jim was a master baker who specialised in pastries and confectioneries and worked locally. A feature of Jim was his mischievous sense of humour and his unbounded energy and these were to last, despite poor health in the last few years of his life, till his death on July 31st 1995. Terry revealed the lively nature of his dad from early on; Michael kept the revelation till much later.

Michael with his mum, Mary

Michael went to the local Catholic Primary School, West Vale, in the neighbouring parish, before Sowerby Bridge had its own Primary School. When a Primary was established by two Sisters of Charity called Sister Petronilla and Sister Nuala, Terry attended and Michael came to the boys' club. Fortunately, each of the Sisters has contributed recollections of those days.

I'm sorry this is so sketchy. I'd love to do justice to the wonderful boy that Michael was. I feel we all owe him so much. We took our Primary School children to Kintbury on quite a few mid-week stays. They benefited enormously from Michael – as we all did.

In August 1953 at the request of Father Austin Roddy PP of Sowerby Bridge, the Sisters of Charity came to start a Catholic School in the presbytery. This was a daunting venture and Fr Roddy needed all the help he could get from his parishioners. One of the most co-operative and enthusiastic families was Mr Lundy's.

At this time the Lundys – Mr and Mrs, Michael, aged 9, and Terry aged seven, had a very happy home which was always full of laughter and song. They were staunch Catholics, participating actively in all parish doings, Mrs. Lundy being a prominent member of the UCM (Union of Catholic Mothers). At great inconvenience the two children were sent a long distance to the Catholic school in the next parish, West Vale.

The presbytery was transformed into a school and the Lundys, who were among the best parish workers, transferred Terry but, as Michael was nearing the 11 + exam, all agreed that he should remain at West Vale school. Michael however joined the Boys' Club and was a most enthusiastic and creative member.

Mr and Mrs Lundy agreed to supply the Catholic school with dinners on three days each week. So Cornish pasties were delivered daily at a moderate cost. On the other days the children had fish and chips. This was only one instance of Mr and Mrs Lundy's Catholic action, and always so cheerfully done.

Alas! In 1955 Mrs Lundy was diagnosed as having cancer and the family was devastated. She was nursed at home and was a wonderfully cheerful patient – still smiling. Her big concern was for the two boys after her death, which she knew to be imminent but which she accepted with heroic faith. A good friend of the family at this time was Ann, Fr Roddy's housekeeper. Mrs Lundy confided in Fr Roddy and asked him to arrange that Ann should marry Mr Lundy and take her place as mother to Michael and Terry. The boys were heartbroken when their mother died.

Eventually Ann did marry Mr Lundy and the two boys did give her a great welcome to their home and their hearts.

After some years the family moved to Bradford and Michael attended the De La Salle Grammar School in Sheffield. Soon after Michael entered the De La Salle Novitiate, Ann died and Mr Lundy came back to live in Halifax. He lived in a small house alone. I went to visit him there. The house was spotless and he proudly showed me a lovely room upstairs, "Michael's room". He looked forward to the days when Michael could come and stay with him for a while. He was a loving father and very proud of Michael.

Sister Petronilla

I first became acquainted with the Lundy family in 1953 when I was sent to teach in Sowerby Bridge, Yorks, in response to an appeal by Fr Austin Roddy, PP who was anxious to provide Catholic education for the younger members of his parish.

Terry Lundy, Michael's younger brother by about two years, was in my class. They both enjoyed a very caring, happy home life with their Mum and Dad. While the two brothers were bosom pals they were very different in temperament. Terry was vivacious and outgoing, a real extrovert. Michael seemed to me to be more of an introvert

Michael, Mary and Terry

with a much more serious attitude to life. Being the older brother, he may have felt it his duty to try to curb some of Terry's love of playing practical jokes. Michael lacked confidence yet he always wanted to be part of the group. He joined wholeheartedly in the fun at the Boys' Club. While quite often I noticed an expression of unsureness on his face, there was also a ready smile when he was accepted and things went well. He was a gentle boy, a bit stocky and sturdy in appearance, with a heart of gold that was full of affection particularly for his mother. Both boys were very attached to her.

It was sad the Autumn day of '55 when one doctor diagnosed that she had cancer. In October of that year she went to Lourdes. En route she called to the school to say 'goodbye' to Terry. It was a very emotional scene. In her heart I felt she knew she would never be cured. Sadly, she died two years later. Although their father did remarry, I think her loss took its emotional toll on the two boys.

I received another assignment in '56 and lost contact with the family, although some years later I had some news of Terry. About ten years ago I met Michael in Chester and re-introduced myself. He told me then of his concerns for his family and I trust he is taking care of them from heaven now.

I have been amazed, looking through various hymnals, at the

number of melodies or lyrics for which Michael has been responsible, helping so many people to praise God and Our Lady. May he rest in peace and enjoy the reward of his labours.

Sister Nuala

So, Sister Petronilla and Sister Nuala give us insights into the tragic early life of Michael and Terry, with interesting arrangements occurring, not least Jim marrying Ann, the parish priest's housekeeper.

The family moved to Bradford and eventually Michael went to De La Salle, Sheffield. We have some of his exercise books (often covered in scribbles and doodles) and a School Report from Summer 1956 when he was in Form 1A (Year 7). His position in the form was 35 on 35. By December 1956 he was in 1B (repeating a year?) and his position was 1 on 36 with not a single day absent. He maintained his efforts and in 3B (Year 9) was again 1 on 35. In those days comments on Reports were generally curt. For Michael the commonest was *Splendid!* He had to cope with so many changes in his life, in this case from a simple primary to Grammar in a hop and step; in a few years another tragedy was to strike. As C. S. Lewis says in *Shadowlands*: "Experience, you're a hard teacher, but by God, we learn!" St Peter was right; from our own sufferings we can learn compassion for others.

Michael, Sheffield uniform

It was at De La Salle Sheffield that Michael flourished and this included his dramatic talents, for he joined the De La Salle College Dramatic Society. In 1957 he was in the cast of *The Taming of the Shrew*, in 1958 performed in *A Midsummer Night's Dream* and in 1959 took part in *Much Ado about Nothing* and a report in the College Annual mentioned in particular the enthusiastic supporting cast: 'I shall single out C. Geoghegan and M. Lundy for their delightful impression of a pair of "young lovers"'. He was a contributor to *Green and Gold* the college magazine (written and edited by past and present members of the college, for their own entertainment and that of their friends) in 1957 offering a study on Mary Queen of Scots entitled *Sheffield's Historical Prisoner* and in 1958 provided a detective story called *The Bistranian Lion*.

While at De La Salle Sheffield he was drawn to the life of the Brothers. Michael took the Habit of the De La Salle Brothers on October 6th 1960, after having spent a year in the Juniorate as an immediate preparation for Novitiate. The Juniorate was in St Cassian's, and the Novitiate in Inglewood (now the Health Hydro!). He took the name Damian, and from now on this is what we shall call him.

Damian, Inglewood Novitiate

His training took him to Germany for the summer holidays and in a letter he makes two interesting remarks that give an insight into the times and into himself: *"I have permission to use the radio whenever I like, and watch the news programme on television, and then one can continue watching if one wants to!"* and *"P.S. No games – it is marvellous."* Quite progressive for 1962! He was in Rheims for a year (1964) and then went to Magdalene College, Cambridge, (1964–67) where he distinguished himself in study and active participation in student life, especially *Footlights*. The reticent introvert spoken of by Sister Nuala had decided to let the "Jim" in him come out. We have a copy of the cast list when he played the part of Corvino in Ben Jonson's *Volpone*. It was his college, Magdalene, that produced an interesting insight into his contribution to the life of the Church worldwide and to his music when they reported his death:

> Dr Michael Lundy (Brother Damian), a Religious Teaching Brother of the De La Salle Brothers, added to his Cambridge degree in English (1967) a BD and a PhD from Manchester. He was responsible for setting up a Religious Renewal Centre in Kintbury, Berkshire, and became prominent as a Catholic activist and hymnologist, an animator and youth counsellor, well-known in European, Irish, Australian, American and Malaysian Catholic circles. His premature death at De La Salle Provincialate in Oxford, aged only fifty-two, is a severe loss to the Church. Some of his hymns are now widely sung, and one or two of them seem likely to endure, for example, 'Walk in the Light' and 'This then is my pray'r'.

While this may appear to be a digression, it further reinforces the dramatic irony of Damian's living. Already touched by the death of Mary, he was only too conscious of his own predicament. It developed in him compassion, sympathy and humility that are the result of reflection, prayer and insight, into the transience and impermanence of human life. His desire was to live fully in the present. He had the ability to be fully NOW! To be engaged with people and activities in a very focused way.

Following his training he was appointed to the Juniorate in St Cassian's (1967–1970) and it was during this time that he made his life-commitment to the De La Salle Brothers with Final Vows on 6th April 1969. In the Juniorate he taught a range of subjects, mainly English and Religious Education, but augmented by a variety of excitements, not least drama and music. Bearing in mind the number of Junior Novices and the isolation of the house, he orchestrated an amazing cultural life for the students and community. To his regret, the regulations of the day made it difficult or impossible for the local people to enjoy the occasions. He looked back with some wry amusement at his Juniorate days when he and the students had been working hard in their free time to produce O *What a Lovely War* and it was the dark time

Damian at St Cassians Juniorate

of winter. The hall was set out with chairs, the guests coming
from Brothers' communities. In rushed Brother Paddy D: "There's
been a phone call from Cardiff. They can't come. They've all got
the 'flu." In typical fashion, Damian then ordered the FRONT
row of seats to be removed! He frequently employed his
mimicking skills to re-create the episode.

His teaching was superb, and his exam results brilliant (bearing
in mind the range that existed in the relatively small numbers in
the Juniorate). Whatever he turned his hand to blossomed and
his creative energy was given free rein; essays, poems, plays,
anecdotes, articles, songs, musicals flowed out of him. Fortunately
he was not required to direct his energies to anything sporting,
for in all the world Damian was the least athletic of men.

From the Juniorate he was appointed to West Park, St Helens, and he was on the staff there from 1970–1975, eventually becoming head of the Religious Education department. He also dived head first into the music and drama productions which had a long tradition of inspirational and highly creative direction and production.

He was daring in the production of *Zigger Zagger* in 1971; a report in the summer magazine wonderingly describing him and his co-producers as "secretaries for the St Helens branch of the Permissive Society?" because "This year the joint ADS of West Park and Notre Dame broke free from the classical strait-jacket and presented the controversial *Zigger Zagger*... When the choice of play was announced, saintly hands rose in horror, the finger of experience was pointed and wise heads shook sadly... This was a little much for some nurtured on the stylish and classical previous productions: *She Stoops to Conquer* and *Quality Street*". The following year (1972) he produced *Oliver*. In 1973 he wrote and produced the musical *The Play of Siegfried* with such stage directions as

> Siegfried's fanfare, followed by steady rhythmic drumbeats. Volker is on the rostrum. Giselher stands in a pool of light centre-stage, or in silhouette, the journey is mimed to the music. As the storm reaches its peak, we see the men tossed from side to side. But Siegfried stands erect steering the ship. As the storm dies down, green and blue light begins to sweep across the stage and we see the surprised faces of the men as they look out towards the new land they are reaching.

The same year he produced an entertainment called *Vintage Music Hall*.

He became involved in the Loughborough Summer Schools in Religious Education, mainly offering workshops on RE in the 6th Form (1974 and 1975). He was in good company for keynote speakers were The Most Reverend Thomas J. Winning and Fr Kevin Nichols. These national conferences were attended by more than 150 people from round the country. Perhaps they were the inspiration for the Catechetical conferences he organised from 1980 onwards. They still continue as the LACE (Lasallian Association for Christian Education) conferences at St Cassian's each May and October. It was while he was at West Park that Damian was elected to the Archdiocesan Pastoral Council and was on the Liturgy Commission, the Schools RE Commission. Perhaps it was just as well he didn't coach rugby and cricket!

His impact at West Park was significant! When news got out of his impending departure to St Cassian's the students wrote a farewell called *Chronomachia*, subtitled *A Masque by divers hands in honour of Bro: Damian Lundy*. It was a comical and serious revue/review of his time at West Park, illustrating the affection in which he was held, their loss at his departure and the wealth of memories he left them by having introduced them to so many different aspects of education and culture. The text is bound between covers of souvenirs of events, activities and experiences he had offered them.

He brought all this richness to St Cassian's when in 1975 he inaugurated with Joe and Dominic the new Retreat Centre. A description of this founding is in another chapter of the book. The move was prompted by Damian's experience of teaching religion in schools and his perception of the limitations this imposed on discussion, choice and development of spirituality. He remained at St Cassian's until 1982 and left a dynamic legacy which has touched, and still touches, the lives of tens of thousands of young people and has offered the opportunity of peer ministry to more than a hundred team members.

Even at St Cassian's his life was touched with tragedy. Just as his mother, Mary, had died suddenly, the family's sadness was compounded when Ann died within two years of his arrival at St Cassian's. He was in the Conference Room on May 2nd 1977 when the phone rang and he was called out to be told the sad news that Ann had died of a heart attack. She was just sisty-six. Damian's own health reflected Mary's in that he later developed a congenital kidney defect which caused cysts to grow in the kidneys, to expand and occasionally burst, causing him great pain.

He knew that eventually one of his kidneys would have to be removed because the swelling would not allow room for two.

In 1983 he received a surprise. His dad, Jim, had proposed to Vi (Violet Allenby Cooper) and they were married on 17th September 1983 in St Mary's Church (The Hidden Gem), Manchester. She was a widow, he a widower. Damian really took to his new mum; she was an outgoing character, very generous and full of fun and she loved to entertain; the games and mischief in that house made it a perpetual party! Vi, a keen cook, pursued one of her ambitions which was to try recipes from different countries. The Beef Olive was magnificent.

Damian was in his element. Vi and Jim visited Kintbury more than once and fell in love with the place. Damian held his dad in great affection and was really upset when Jim had a number of strokes which compounded his major problem of emphysema and lung cancer. Jim had the knack of keeping that sparkle in the eyes even when initially he could not speak because of the effects of the stroke. On one occasion Benet took Damian to see Jim in Halifax General Hospital and on arrival the nurses indicated that Jim was not in a good fettle (he wasn't allowed to smoke). The ward was circular in design and there was Jim sitting up in bed looking grim. He looked up, saw Damian, Vi and Benet, and all Benet did was pretend to puff on a cigarette. Jim's face lit up, his eyes sparkled and he laughed a silent deep laugh. He saw the irony of his situation and was happy to chuckle at it. It was a feature Damian inherited too. Ben Foy also took Damian to see Jim and he has a rather sad recollection of the impact the visit had on Damian:

> Taking him to see his father – seriously ill in hospital – was the only occasion when I saw Damian so deeply upset that he was completely lost for words. He sat for two or three hours at the bedside holding his Dad's hand quite distressed. Although he put on a brave face for his stepmother – who naturally insisted on feeding us – he wept quietly in the car on the way back to Manchester.

While "Kintbury" (1975–1982) was going on, Damian was involved in a host of other things. Gerard Rummery, a key international figure in the Brothers, arranged for Damian to come to Australia in the summer of 1976 to see the Retreat Centre at Cronulla in Sydney which had been running for some years. Gerard had been invited by the National Catechetical Commission to arrange a series of workshops in various dioceses to prepare for the 1977 Roman Synod on *Catechesis in Our Time*. The visit was arranged for June, July and early August. Damian was able to spend some two weeks in the Cronulla Retreat Centre and then together he and Gerard spent the next 8-9 weeks in Australia and New Zealand working mainly with teachers and adults who were interested in the religious education of young people. They also presented a week together in the National Pastoral Centre in Melbourne.

Adult formation, catechesis and training was an area into which Damian was to develop his gifts further, and his Australian experience helped to give him a taste for this. He became an

Members of the Catechetical Commission.
Israel Neri, Gerard Rummery, Damian Lundy and Teodolo Garcia Redidor.
Slopes of Mt. Subasio, Assisi.

international figure and it is astonishing how many different countries welcomed him and found him original and inventive.

His skill in adapting, writing and modifying music and song for young adolescents which culminated in the three volumes of *Songs of the Spirit* first revealed itself during his time of working in the Juniorate at Kintbury in the late 1960's. His gift had already been refined by having to have them sung by croaky-voiced adolescents! By the late 1970's, however, especially through his work with Brother Joseph Hendron in the Pastoral Centre at Kintbury after 1975, he had already been profoundly influenced by his contact with the charismatic movement and by leading figures in it. This transformation was clearly in process in him when he came to make the Brothers' Renewal Programme in Rome in the first three months of 1979. No one who made that session will easily forget Damian leading *Bind us Together* and generally getting things moving.

Damian had the insight and sensitivity to know when to move on. His vision for St Cassian's was underway and could confidently be left in the hands of others. He still maintained an intense interest in the people, the place and the work, but interfere he would not. His main call was for those now in charge to continue to develop the centre and to respond to new spiritual needs as enunciated by the young people themselves. Often he was being called to a new ministry, and he had the facility to be devoted very much to the "present" ministry or moment.

He moved to further study, his whole self needing a fresh challenge. It also gave him space for himself which the previous seven years had severely limited. In 1982 he was involved in the organisation and content of the Ninian Park Papal visit. The designation on his security pass was "Announcer"! That he was asked to be part of it comes as no surprise; he was probably more in touch with young people than anyone else in the country. That he had the time to do it is astonishing. But he loved a challenge and it gave great scope to his creativity, his insights, his music and above all Lasallian Resource, the music and choir group that were the living expression of renewal through music. The invitation to Damian – and Lasallian Resource – to lead the music at the Youth event at Ninian Park during the Pope's visit took place as a consequence of his being so well known to the organisers of the event – through Charismatic Renewal – and to the Catholic Youth Service who were responsible for the event. This was an occasion which he was very happy about – despite becoming quite exhausted by the energy which he expended.

He wrote for significant periodicals, for example *The Way* (*The Beginnings of Prayer*), and contributed regularly to it; and wrote for the De La Salle Brothers' *Newsletter*. With Dom Edmund Flood OSB, he was co-editor of *The Sower* (A Quarterly Magazine on Christian Formation founded by Fr Drinkwater whom Damian hugely admired and took as his inspiration). While in Australia he appeared on television, the subject of the interview being *Where God Hides*. He also wrote *To Grow in Christ, A Plan for Prayer* which is firmly founded on scripture. A further volume, *What's the Point of It All?*, was an extremely sensitive response to his experience at St Cassian's; he did not like the title but it was imposed on him by the publishers as part of a series. Towards the end of his life (1995) he collaborated with Dom Christopher Jamison OSB and Sister Louisa Poole SSL in a book entitled *To Live is to Change: a way of reading Vatican II*. The launch of the book took place at Vaughan House behind Westminster Cathedral and Archbishop Worlock endorsed the occasion, as did Bishop Konstant and Sister Dorothy Bell. The Archbishop was happy to remind those gathered at the launch that he was the sole member of the Hierarchy of England and Wales who had attended all the sessions of the Second Vatican Council. He also suggested a modification of the subtitle to the book (*a way*) for the original was simply: *How to...* The book made accessible to parishes and Sixth Form students in particular the themes, teaching and writings of the Second Vatican Council. The title, taken from John Henry Newman, was a significant one for Damian, for his life had seen many changes, some of them painful. But he had also discovered that exploration in the light of the gospel and in the Holy Spirit brought real benefits for young people and adults alike.

He liked to challenge his Brothers too, for in the heady days after Vatican II he began an in-house discussion publication called *SPARK*, and he was only 24 at the time. Here is an extract from the first editorial:

> All the material contained in this first issue of *SPARK* is based on the theme "A Changing Institute". The second issue will be based on the same theme. Much of what is said will be controversial. *SPARK* aims to stimulate its readers, as well as to inform them – it invites them all to take part, not as passive spectators but as active partners in a shared action. The Editor will be glad to print correspondence, and hopes that this will be abundant and vigorous.

He was ever alert, curious, and happy to follow the encouragement of Lonergan: if you are not satisfied with the answer, ask another question. On INSET days he would always pose significant questions to staff, probing their values and relationships. He teased out mission statements and probed high-sounding phrases in prospectuses. He challenged:

> You do not control a thing by pretending it doesn't exist, nor by simply ignoring it. It is the complacent 'untouchables' – the sleepers unmoving and unmoved – who are most dangerous, not those who are naturally cautious and conservative. But as Rosemary Haughton puts it wisely, "Remove from the Christian message its ability to shock and Christianity… is altogether destroyed." So, to find and keep and pass on the sense of excitement of 'SHOCK' not too self-consciously, but naturally, as it arises from our experience of tension – is essential, if we are to be alive and keep alive.

SPARK certainly maintained the experience of tension. Its life span was short, but it could not be avoided.

> We don't KNOW exactly what is happening to us, or even where we are going. Our recognition of the meaning and value of the experience will become clearer and more defined as we

respond to it. We must learn to respond, by taking risks, by groping and comparing and testing. This is what *SPARK* is for."

We hope that *SPARK 4* will appear in the autumn and that the material it contains (especially the correspondence) will develop and extend, as well as challenge, some of the ideas presented in this issue. It will also contain some personal impressions of the August Session of our District Chapter. As this is likely to be only the *first* session, the discussion is likely to be still hot. May *SPARK* help to keep it that way.

His BD studies at Manchester University, begun in 1983, were punctuated by a year in Rome on the Brothers' International Rule Commission (1984–85) which introduced him to many of the foremost thinkers in the De La Salle Institute. That he was among them says much, though his natural humility made little of it.

Damian's studies in Manchester up to 1988 for his PhD helped him to develop his insights and ideas on the need for adult catechesis and his thesis is on this very topic. Such is its popularity that more than 200 requests have been made to use it for reading and research. When he had completed his doctorate he was invited by the Bishops' Conference to join the National Project from 1988 to 1992. It was a time of research, testing, development, imagination, creativity and controversy. The last because the nature of the project highlighted the need for change, for a new approach to catechesis in schools and in parishes. Damian's own research had also opened his eyes to the needs of adult catechesis. Not everyone in the Catholic community was of a similar opinion. He worked very closely with Fr Jim Gallagher, Sr Bernadette and Anne White and their insights are to be found later in the book.

In 1992 he was elected to the Provincial Team of the De La Salle Brothers. For many years he had been fully involved in the life of the Province: Chapters, Councils, Formation teams, Conference organiser and member of Commissions. But now he was asked to take on specific responsibility for the pastoral and educational care of the De La Salle organisation in Great Britain and abroad. In terms of experience he had so much to draw on. Just as he challenged everyone he met, in just the way they needed, so also as a member of the Team he challenged the others – Tom and Benet, the Council, staffs in schools and Brothers in communities. He promoted a new style of Chapter for the Brothers and their partners, making all aspects of life relevant to ministry and mission. He promoted a joint conference at All Saints Pastoral Centre on The Christian School, a collaboration between those from the De La Salle tradition and those from the Christian Brothers' and their staffs. He also helped to run seminars for schools on creative religious education, pastoral care and on prayer. His forte was to recognise expertise "in house" and to enable those so gifted to express their gifts for others. He also took to heart the need to be challenged constantly and, with a sureness of judgement, invited guests and experts from outside the "family" to enlighten, challenge, put to the test. His approach to all things was inclusive, embracing those who disagreed with him as much as those who were taken by what he said and did. In 1994 he led a day with Ruth Duckworth for the religious of Westminster Diocese, the theme being preparation for the Synod on the Consecrated Life.

His move from Kensington to Oxford enabled him to become involved in music and liturgy in Sacred Heart parish, Blackbird Leys, and he felt very much at home in the community there where he was welcomed and encouraged. The twin church was in Littlemore, the home of Cardinal Newman, and the Newman Centre was cared for by the Sisters of the Work. Damian got to know the Sisters well, and through them became more closely acquainted with Cardinal Newman's writings and influence. With Benet he also helped to organise training days for parish catechists and reunion sessions for young people who had recently been confirmed. He was ever involved with people, first hand.

He was a lively and cheerful character to live with and was a constant source of fun and banter. He was a good cook, too, and was happy to prepare an evening meal on Saturdays from time to time – usually a pasta with delicious sauce.

In late summer of 1991 Damian was invited to join a CAFOD factfinding mission to Central America; he accepted and visited

Guatemala, El Salvador and Nicaragua. It was a harrowing, humbling and transfiguring experience. The objective of the visit was "to see how, in spite of the situation, people keep up their spirits and go forward", and in each of these countries the situation was precarious. His notes recall his preparation: "you breathe fear in the air in Central America", and he observed stark contrasts: poverty, repression, political instability, injustice, civil war, earthquakes, volcanoes, mountains and staggering beauty in an area where the few own so much. He witnessed massive repression, overt persecution and incredible faith; a preferential option for the poor so strong that "it is more appropriate to die than to leave". In El Salvador he learned of 'Blowtorch Bob' whose call was "Be a patriot. Kill a priest." He came to understand more about the life and death of Bishop Oscar Romero *Profeta y Martir*. He visited the Catholic University where the six Jesuits and two women were shot. He learned of the invitation: "Let your heart be broken – it will change your view of the world." He learned of the poor woman whose daughter and niece had been decapitated. She went to Romero for comfort and ended up comforting him. "To me you give the wild ox's strength". The power of the scriptures permeates his appreciation of the work of the poor in supporting each other. He bore witness to the women in El Salvador who stood up for the 8,000 'disappeared' and protested at the 74,000 killed. Their offices were bombed four times. "All the women we met," he records, "had been raped and tortured." It gave a new meaning to "Zeal for your house has devoured me." He met the most incredible faith, resilience and hope; the main source materials for groups meeting in parishes for biblical reflection to consider their situation were *Exodus* and the *Prophetic* Books. The most cryptic note reads: Music: 'You are the God of the poor'. Discuss. A Taizé chant took on new meaning: "No se desmayes, ni se aflites, porque Dios esta contigo" (Do not be downhearted or discouraged, because God is with you).

For some time after his return from Central America he was feeling poorly, mainly a stomach complaint that would not go away. He visited the doctor several times from the end of October, and eventually asked whether it was anything he might have picked up while abroad. The doctor smilingly said it was just as likely to be London that provided the problem. Still the illness went on and one day Benet met Damian coming off the tube at Gloucester Road; Damian looked dreadful. He went to the doctor again, but this time it was a *locum* (a former student from a Brother's school). It was his opinion that the symptoms might be masking something else and arranged for tests. Before the tests took place Damian suffered a heart attack on Friday 7th February and was taken to Queen Mary Hospital Paddington. Twice in 1992 the doctors tried an angioplasty (an attempt to widen the artery) without success, so a multiple heart bypass operation was arranged for 14th May 1993. Unfortunately the poor state of his kidneys meant he could not cope with the toxins from the operation and he suffered severe kidney failure and had to be put on dialysis. His life changed radically.

Initially three times a week he was on haemodialysis (on computerised machines that filtered his blood) at the Churchill Hospital in Oxford, so he was limited in what he could do, where and when. His sessions were always late evening because he had transport and lived locally, for the dialysis centre catered for more than twelve health areas. So he would go in at about 7.0 p.m. and depending on how smoothly the day sessions had gone, would be out at midnight or 1.0 a.m. Anton, one of his regular chauffeurs, writes: "He found this taxing and uncongenial. His distress at this, meekly borne, was more impressive than any heroic indifference would have been". He kept himself occupied during the sessions, mainly by reading, and he soon made an impression. Anton writes again:

> One of the nurses was efficient, rather uncommunicative, and professedly indifferent to religion and hocus pocus. She made light of Damian's work as she saw it – 2 days per week: Saturday to prepare the sermon and Sunday to give it! Gradually and good humouredly, Damian described the reality and broke down the resistance. His charm penetrated even his distress. She became more relaxed and always good for a pleasant chat.

She was, unpredictably, married to a Catholic Spaniard. They took their holidays in Spain. From there she wrote a card to Damian at the Unit, giving him to understand that, with more good will than understanding, she had gone into a Church with her husband and had set a candle for his intentions. On her return she brought Damian some candles (red ones) and after the usual banter Damian teased her with, "You do realise that red candles are used only at funerals!" She replied without batting an eyelid: "I wouldn't worry I pinched them anyway." He missed her when he changed his dialysis system.

Damian very much appreciated the care he received at the Dialysis Unit, and he was astonished at the nature of the process. He wrote to Gerard on one occasion: "Incredibly, last week in two sessions of dialysis they removed seven pounds weight of impurities which the kidneys had failed to dispose of… I never thought it was possible to lose seven pounds weight in six hours. If only dieting were as easy!"

Not everything went smoothly. On occasions his blood pressure would drop dramatically and he would go into a faint. Once this happened when he was being taken back to a ward on a wheelchair. The porter, trained to respond by seeking the nearest nursing help, immediately pushed Damian into the nearest ward: Gynaecology!

His veins were turning to string and the staff were finding it increasingly difficult to insert the needles for good flow, three attempts at inserting a fistula (a gortex graft in the forearm) having failed. So he had to have neck lines surgically inserted: painful, grossly obvious and uncomfortable. Damian referred to them as his gin-and-tonic lines. Unfortunately, he had picked up a serious infection through the lines and the virus had seeded itself in a valve in his heart. The surgeons said there were two options: massive bombardment with antibiotics or another heart operation. Damian opted for the antibiotics and for seven weeks endured continuous drips. The side effects are hard to imagine. His only comfort was to sit and stare at nothing; eventually a small TV was brought to his room (though he was a scant watcher usually) and during this time the peak viewing was the Conservative Party Conference. His comment at the end of this enlightening experience was "I think I have become more assertive". The illness took its toll and he was unable to get away for a break in the summer. Damian's creativity took over: he spent a week visiting the cinema, relaxed and occasionally intellectually challenged.

After an extended time on haemodialysis (now four times a week and with an extra hour) it was suggested that he might change to a different form: CAPD (Continuous Ambulatory Peritoneal Dialysis) which the person does at home. It involved the insertion of a catheter into the peritoneum to enable the lining to act as a filter. The system meant putting (via the tube) a litre of glucose solution into the abdomen, waiting three to four hours and then draining it out; after which another litre was inserted. This happened four times a day, every day; continuous the title, continuous the process. After the operation to insert the catheter Damian was in some considerable pain, especially when he laughed. He received no sympathy from the nurses! "That," they said with a knowing grin, "is the nearest you'll get to childbirth pains!" "In that case, thank God I'm a man!" came the wincing reply, for he could not but laugh at his own inconvenience.

The demands of this type of dialysis were time consuming, though it gave a certain freedom which the other did not. Providing he took his equipment with him he could travel and stay overnight. He could eat a wider range of foods since the regular dialysis got rid of a build up of toxins. The one thing he was advised of was scrupulous hygiene, for the main danger was infection through the catheter and peritonitis.

He tried a couple of times to venture on holiday. He had been invited by Brother Herman Lombaerts (one of his close friends in catechetics) to go over to Belgium and stay for a while, and to have a look at some developments. The company which regularly delivered his glucose solution had a European Service too and, given three weeks notice, would arrange for delivery to his door in Belgium. Done! The flight was arranged and Damian, delighted, prepared for the adventure. On the morning of the flight he received an urgent phone call from his hosts to say that none of the fluid had been delivered. Frantic phone calls, company promised, etc. He took one spare bag with him. He arrived *chez* Herman: nothing. He used his one bag and waited. Nothing. Fortunately Herman's sister was a dialysis nurse (O Providence!) and arranged an emergency delivery for him. The anxiety, the very cold weather and the journey took their toll of Damian and he spent the whole time ill in bed. He was bitterly disappointed for he had looked forward to the change and to the intellectual challenge any meeting with Herman would bring.

In August of 1996 Damian asked Benet if he would be willing to go on holiday with him to Rhiw, the Brothers' house in North Wales. With the car it would be possible to take a week's supply of dialysis fluid and his equipment, though whenever asked for his requirements he always said "Just a hook" (to hang the bag on). It was a glorious August and they went out every day, visiting, relaxing, enjoying the scenery. A favourite was Talhenbont Hall (*Plas Talhenbont*) with its ducks and geese, white pheasants (Daz and Omo) and peacocks (fed by hand) and the immobile horse. There was fun in the craft area (called the Woodworm), with buying of presents including a dozen finger mice. Tea was taken in the front lounge on the sofas, the hostess a great conversationalist. They visited Porthmeirion on a spectacular summer's day. But the highlight was the trip into Snowdonia (memories of Austria and mountain climbing?) and the wonderful sight of Damian, drip on its stand high in the air, dialysing in the shadow of Snowdon much to the astonishment of passers-by in cars and coaches. The experience lifted his spirits.

In November of that year Damian was asked to go to Rome for an international meeting and he readily accepted. This time the arrangement for delivery of the dialysis fluid went without a hitch. He really enjoyed the challenge and Rome, for his previous stays in Rome on the Rule Commission had given him a great love for the place, the culture, the people, the *joie de vivre*. Ben Foy who attended the *Colloquium* wrote this:

My final experience with Damian was when we went to Rome together for a *Colloquium* in the Mother House. We sat together several times whilst he did his dialysis. He was really delighted that he was able to be present for the *Colloquium* on Continuing Formation because it had been possible to arrange the supplies necessary for dialysis. He was happy to be able to take part – and feel that he was able to contribute. The only thing he felt unable to do was to take part in the Rome-by-night tour – but thought it a source of great amusement to have the luminescent cap which the leaders provided for those who were taking part! He was particularly delighted to be invited to stay on in Rome for a few days holiday. When I left him he asked me to bring his cap and some of his papers for the conference home for him and we arranged to meet the following week. My final memory of him was of a contented person, at peace with himself, with others and with God – and looking to what we could develop for the future, from what we had learned from the *Colloquium*.

All went well until the day of his return when he began to feel ill. On his return to England he went directly from the airport to the Churchill Hospital in Oxford; he never recovered and died on December 9th 1996.

Damian recognised only too well the fragility of his life. It gave a poignancy to all he did.

His funeral Mass was celebrated in Dominic Barber Church in Littlemore and crowds turned up to sing and pray and reminisce. It was a fitting tribute to such a multifaceted man. He was buried on Monday December 16th in Wolvercote Cemetery, Oxford, in a plot recently purchased by the Brothers, and his grave is next to Peter Hebblethwaite. We await their joint article in *The Tablet!*

His memory is alive and well. He had been invited to inaugurate a new Catechetical Centre in the Nottingham diocese shortly before his death; three national groups were keen to arrange the celebration of his life at the Mass in Our Lady of Victories, Kensington; the inaugural Damian Lundy Memorial Lecture, launched by CATSC (Catholic Association of Teachers, Schools and Colleges) on June 20th 1998, was given by John Sullivan; in

September 2000 St Cassian's Centre will celebrate twenty-five years of its life and ministry, with the memory of Damian as central to it; in January 1999 the new Garden Room at St Cassian's was opened in memory of him; LACE, the support conference for staff and chaplains continues under the care of Brother Terence Collins; his *Songs* are sung, his thesis read, his influence lived daily in thousands of lives. Damian loved to reflect on the quotation from *Gaudium et Spes*: "The future of humanity lies in the hands of those who are strong enough to provide coming generations with reasons for living and hoping." His whole life was inspired by the search to offer young people and adults these deep reasons. Read on for further inspiration.

3 | Damian: Teacher, Communicator, Writer...

The title of this chapter has no full stop because such a final piece of punctuation fails to do justice to the various titles which could be attributed to Damian. He connected with people in so many different ways without ever having to stand on the dignity of his academic degrees or his extraordinary international experience. Here are some of the impressions of the 'teacher', 'communicator', and 'writer' shared by some very different people who met him.

> My mind is full of pictures of Damian from the first time I accompanied some sixth-formers [to Kintbury] and met this amazing Tweedledum figure in an enormous Oxfam cardigan! Some time later when he had slimmed considerably, I walked past him, pretending not to see him, until brought to a halt by his indignant 'Heh! Heh!' (What self-discipline he had to have – a supper of two measly sticks of celery while surrounded by teenagers wolfing huge platefuls)… Damian brought knowledge, scholarship together with joy and encouragement to everyone he met.

> Damian was the driving force on so many fronts – indeed you often ended up on his waggon not quite remembering boarding it. He was that unique combination of audience-holding, charismatic and yet humble (almost shy) individual. His presence affected many people and his light burned brightly – perhaps too brightly for his body to cope with.

For me and for countless young people, Damian was Kintbury. His special gifts, charismatic personality, and genuine goodness made the experience of being at Kintbury one that literally changed their lives.

More than anything else Damian helped me to love poetry, and I can't read Gerard Manley Hopkins or A.E. Houseman without thinking of his lessons, and the sheer weight of his enthusiasm for literature.

Since the news came I haven't come to the end of counting the many gifts Damian shared with me among so many of his contributions to community and religious living, to education and religious formation, to liturgy, literature, drama and music and by all the things he inspired in me and others – and above and away beyond all by the frank affection and *joie de vivre* he spread all around him. *(Joan Williams)*

The above tributes and countless others from those who knew Damian in his various guises – teacher of literature, welcoming host at Kintbury, presenter to staff development days, speaker at religious education conferences, leader of workshops on changes in religious life, international lecturer, researcher on the National Project – simply remind us what a richly engaging personality he had. Perhaps, however, it is possible to see certain enduring aspects which seemed to run through everything he did as teacher, friend, communicator – as Damian!

First, and possibly most importantly, he was someone who related easily and naturally to all those with whom he came in contact no matter their age, background or position. His introduction to Kintbury groups was simple and direct, "I'm Damian!" He was as much at his ease with young children as he was with his literature students, his actors in his drama productions, Kintbury participants preparing a liturgy, the musicians who formed Lasallian Resource, his university professors and the Brothers of his own Institute. This aspect of his personality was, as one of the above quotations so perceptively pointed out, related to his very real humility, his truthful assessment of himself: he always felt there was something more to be discovered by being in contact with other people and by being really present to them. One of the tributes paid to his memory notes that *"Damian gave witness to the rare virtue of humility, and his understanding of service to others was imbued with the De La Salle spirit."*

Second, Damian was someone who believed in dialogue and who practised it in everything he did. The word for him was not simply a handy catchphrase: it meant speaking, and listening, and speaking again because he had listened. His style of presenting anything was to engage his audience in the process by his invitatory style of presentation, by his eye contact with those present, by his questions, by his willingness to entertain the answers given, by his frequent insistence on things to be written down, points to be discussed with others and by his attempt to establish a common position as the fruit of the diverse activities which he directed. Dialogue with Damian was not static: it always moved on because he really listened to what others said and this determined what he said next. Add to these enduring and endearing characteristics the richness of his own broad education through profound scholarship, membership of a worldwide congregation, his experience of working in many other countries, his openness to the world around him, and you begin to appreciate just why he was so special.

Damian, the teacher

Damian was a gifted teacher of literature, a tribute paid to him by so many people who still find themselves inspired by the way he opened up the vast world of literature for them. This could have been expected from his undergraduate studies in literature at Cambridge. But Damian became, through his training as a Brother, his Kintbury experiences and the broad vision opened up for him by practical experience of his membership of a world-wide Institute, an outstanding religious educator, not simply a skilled practitioner but someone who left others richer from their experience of working *with* him. For that was his style: he worked *with* others so that all learned together. Among the many written tributes paid to his memory, the following express not only their appreciation of the man, the De La Salle Brother, but also the recognition of the impact which he made through so many different kinds of sessions with school staffs and other communities in direct contact with the young.

We are very grateful for the priceless support he offered us as a school, particularly the in-service opportunities for staff, and more recently, for the central role he played in the induction of our Sixth Formers. As is his wont, he quickly established a good rapport with a religiously mixed ability body of some 300, and made a considerable impact in such a short time.
We shall miss his understated talents, his openness, warmth and support greatly and we give thanks for his life and his example. He touched our hearts and we are all the richer for it. *(Tony McCaffery, St. Peter's Bournemouth)*

He provided a wonderful inset for me in my school – his inspiration was just something else. I was talking to him only a couple of weeks ago about the conference in January – even that short call left me inspired. *(Bernardette Bleasedale)*

(Damian's) spirit very much lives on in the hearts of so many of us who were privileged to know him and work with him... I know of few people who have contributed more to bringing alive the spirit of Vatican II in the English Church. He made theory, religious education, scriptures, prayer and liturgy interesting, relevant and fun. What a gift! *(Francis Hall, Christian Brothers)*

Very recently he facilitated a day for teachers in a school... and it was a wonderful day... He was a reminder of the true values of education and his love and enthusiasm for his work were always very obvious. *(Presentation Sisters)*

He led an outstanding day for us which helped focus the staff and our mission as a Catholic Sixth Form College. On a personal note, I worked with him at West Park Grammar School for two years and then our paths crossed on many occasions in different places including Kintbury. *(Tony Andrews, Xaverian, Manchester)*

He was indeed a truly great man who put his considerable talents, imagination and wit at the service of the Institute and the Lasallian mission... His death touches me very deeply as well. We forged a wonderful relationship in Rome as we worked together on the Rule commission. *(Luke Salm)*

Damian, the writer

If, as the French expression has it, *Le style c'est l'homme*, we can appreciate many of these characteristics of Damian as "teacher, communicator and writer" in a special way by looking at what he left us in his writings. Apart from a number of articles and his academic writings treated elsewhere in this book, Damian's three books were *To Grow in Christ* in 1980, *Growing into Faith* (with Gerard Rummery) in 1982, and *To Live is to Change* (with Christopher Jamieson OSB & Louisa Poole SSL) in 1995.

The little book called *What's the Point of it All?*, published in 1992, is particularly valuable in providing us with some remarkable insights into Damian's own life and the way in which he could look back at the passage of God in his own life through his relationship with others. The provocative title reminds us that we all ask this kind of question at various times in our lives. Damian's deep interest in faith as a dynamic gift and his deep love for the document on the Church called *Gaudium et Spes* [Joy and Hope], leads him to suggest that

> "unless I ask it, I cannot grow into mature faith... The Second Vatican Council noted that for twentieth century Christians who share the joys, hopes, griefs and anxieties of their fellow men and women, life in the world today raises the question with a special intensity... it challenges me to get clearer about my reasons for living and hoping, so that I can be ready to share them with others."

This statement comes as no surprise to those who knew him so well since, as will be pointed out in the chapter on Damian as a *practical mystic*, this willingness, even compulsion, to share what he himself had contemplated, was fundamental to what he came to see was his ministry to others.

Six of the eight separate chapters of *What's the Point of it All?* begin from the present, the here and now of this world. Each tells the story of a young man or young woman whom Damian had come to know, sometimes in the most unexpected ways. In the two other chapters, Damian reflects on Francis of Assisi and on one of the Dietrich Bonhoeffer letters written from prison just about the time Damian was born. Each story leads Damian to reflect on particular passages or incidents from Scripture. At the end of each chapter there is a section called FOR PRAYER AND REFLECTION in which Damian involves the reader in some observations and questions which help to bring the whole topic back to the personal and the present.

In the opening chapter, his meeting with Donald, orphaned through a series of tragic events, leads him to share with this young man the story of Job, to plumb with him the depths of suffering. As you read the text you realise very quickly that this is no attempt to allow Donald to wallow in well meant sympathy: it is a journey in which Damian is guide and companion to the expression of profound truths about life and suffering which they deepen together. The Donald who finishes this reading with Damian has been helped to move a long way from the young man who *"knew that there was a such a book* [of Job] *in the Bible."* But it does not finish there. The four questions FOR PRAYER AND REFLECTION move the story back to the reader's own life: the dialogue is now to continue. All who shared a Kintbury session or a workshop with Damian find themselves in familiar territory.

The Simon of the second chapter is the young man whose Kintbury experience (which in his case includes receiving rebuke for some over enthusiastic hugging!) leads him to become active with other young people in his parish. He develops his personal prayer, discovers *The Imitation of Christ*, and above all, comes to a deeper Christian understanding of how he can help his spastic sister by taking her for walks. The letter is quite moving to read. From this down-to-earth example, Damian moves through a wonderful *coda*, because *When God comes into your life, you start to change. All your relationships are affected. Your eyes are opened*

*to the amazing grace of God's presence. What happened to Simon
has happened to many.*

and he makes the connection,

> It happened to Saul of Tarsus, turning him into the greatest
> Christian missionary, a man of passionate and untiring zeal.

The third question FOR PRAYER AND REFLECTION makes use of the
story of John Newton and the hymn *Amazing Grace* by showing
the connection between Newton's discovery of the *Imitation of
Christ* and Simon's own discovery of the same text. Damian loved
Amazing Grace both for its haunting melody and the power of
some of its simple words. He particularly relished the contrast of
lost and *found, blind* and *see*, about which he had written in his
Easter Sunday prayer (No. 47) in *To Grow in Christ.*

Damian's third chapter is on the man born blind in the 9th
chapter of John's Gospel. The present tense this time is Damian's
recollection of John Hull, the blind theologian, whom he had
first met at the James Fowler workshop which Damian had helped
to organise at Newman College, Birmingham. Some years later
Damian saw the BBC's *Everyman* programme on John Hull's
autobiography and it is some moving excerpts from this book
which introduce the chapter. He then allows the Gospel text to
speak for itself before suggesting a number of important reflections
on the event and on the questions posed by the disciples to Jesus.

Some readers of these memories of Damian have been
privileged to follow this particular workshop on the *Man born
blind* with him. His use of the text and the reflections which he
develops from it are certainly among the finest things he ever
presented and it is no surprise to find this master-teacher returning
to suggest a meditative reflection on John Hull's exquisite
appropriation of Psalm 139.

The longest and most worked out chapter of the book is
Damian's reflection on chapters 20 and 21 of John's Gospel. Some
of these are the same elements which he had already treated in
the 48th and 49th days of his little book, *To Grow in Christ.* In

practice, he examines four post-Resurrection Gospel stories and appends separate PRAYER AND REFLECTION questions after each story. He sees in these stories profound reasons *"for living and hoping,"* a phrase which is to reappear in his reflections on the 4th story. The title, *To live in the light of the Resurrection*, is taken from one of the letters from Bonhoeffer's *Letters and Papers from Prison*, a book in which Damian found a number of important reflections, because they date from around the time of his own birth and remind him of the world into which he was born.

It is worth noting that these studies from John's Gospel are the fruit of his own scholarship at Manchester University. Because he had to learn New Testament Greek in his study of this Gospel, he brought a sense of rediscovery to what were already familiar texts as he was helped by his own teachers to probe the deeper meanings behind the words. It is this sense of excitement which gives these 3rd and 4th chapters a particularly *Damianesque* flavour: he is sharing his own enthusiasm!

The next chapter is on Francis of Assisi. Damian's "discovery" of Francis was heightened by his experiences in Rome in 1979 as has already been referred to in this biography. Suffice it to say that Damian's retelling of the Francis story becomes for the reader a series of challenges about being the presence of Christ in today's world.

The sixth chapter begins with the strange story of Jane, *"a very disturbed person, physically and psychologically handicapped, in a wheelchair, rejected as a child by her parents."* A mutual friend had suggested to Jane that she might like to speak with Damian; Damian had accepted without ever imagining just what he was being asked to get into. The story is deeply moving as there are hesitations and changed appointments until the day when Jane finally comes. Damian, on his own admission, does nothing except push Jane around in her wheelchair for an hour in the Berkshire countryside, listening to her but saying practically nothing that he can recall. It is a Kintbury *Emmaus walk* with a difference! She refuses to come in for a meal and goes away, promising to write. Jane's letter is deeply moving, a series of thank yous *"for showing me that God loves the very me that I have so despised."*

Even in the little that we are told, however, we can glimpse something of Damian, something which Jane herself in some way came to understand: his willingness to listen, to be non-judgemental, to offer reasons for living and hoping. Notice that Damian calls Jane's letter his "eucharistic postcard." The chapter develops some important consoling thoughts from John's Gospel and from Paul to the Romans, but this is simply a way of leading to a brilliant analysis and reflection on some of the most important ideas of the mystic, Julian of Norwich, some of whose ideas he had already treated in the 49th prayer of *To Grow in Christ*. As always, the PRAYER AND REFLECTION questions address the basic ideas in a very personal way. Damian's particular gift as a communicator was his ability to ask the provocative question which helped his present day readers to think along with the ideas of a 14th century mystic! The dialogue in this sense was always being prolonged beyond the stage of exposition.

The hero of the final chapter is Archbishop Romero as Damian is led to reflect on his experience of visiting El Salvador along with a CAFOD study group in 1991. It touches on some important themes from the Book of Revelation but the chapter is especially directed to the theme of hope. In the FOR PRAYER AND REFLECTION Damian stresses this aspect:

> My visit to El Salvador in 1991 renewed my sense of hope. Many aspects of it sickened and distressed me, but the overall effect was that my faith, hope, love and joy were strengthened.

The *Sharing the Darkness* chapter is one of the most intimate pieces of self-revelation which we are privileged to have from Damian. It is, as he acknowledges, a different kind of chapter but it is concerned with the same fundamental question as all the others: *what is the point of it all?* In this case, however, the question is one with which Damian himself is confronted as he has to learn to live with failure. The narrative enables the reader to feel something of the "almost" which Clive seems to reach, it hints at the feeling that perhaps Damian will succeed. But that is not what happens, and Damian, at his most personal, admits that with both Tony and Clive, *I know that I failed to teach them very much. They rejected what I offered them, but they taught me a lot about myself.*

Later in the chapter he is led to acknowledge that "*the relationships on which I reflect in the two poems were difficult and testing and incomplete.*" Perhaps that is why the poem *For Tony* remains such an important poem for us all. It is about Tony, but it is also very much about Damian and about a hurt which could only be expressed through the outpouring which is the poem itself.

The story of Clive is a Kintbury story of a different kind. It is moving and in some ways, deeply disturbing, but some parents and many teachers know of other Clives. What may be most important about this chapter is the reflection by Damian which follows:

> When I talk of my 'sharing the darkness', Tony's darkness, Clive's darkness, I mean it. I'm not being rhetorical. I have a real sense of failure. You see, I feel unable to share my deepest sense with anyone, and yet I am so moved when others take me into their confidence and develop a relationship in faith and love… These young people have taught me so much, because they've made me ask myself some fundamental questions. I wanted 'to untie them and let them go free' but I discovered my own weakness, my inability to untie not only their knots but also my own.

In some ways, this is the true Damian, the teacher, the communicator, the man of dialogue who finds that the other person has not listened or is unwilling to listen. It is not a question of improving his technique. What he realises is that the other has refused to continue the dialogue and has turned away. His tears are not really just for Tony: they are also for himself, for his own failure in not being able to engage the one who has walked away. But they are not tears of frustration: they are the fruit of the love, the yearning to help Tony and Clive discover the God who loves them.

It is worth noting that the examples used in *What's the point of it all?* confirm what has been already said about Damian earlier in this chapter: he was the man of dialogue, someone who listened and learned, someone who reflected deeply on the young people whom he always declared himself "privileged" to have met. His reflections are always strained through the filter of his own faith and zeal. He speaks of some of his thank you letters as "eucharistic", no idle term for him but a profound recognition that the moments with this particular person had become, in shared faith, Emmaus moments of personal discovery. But the prevailing mood is often one of humility, a kind of personal wonderment at the power of God's grace which had shone through the relationship.

As we have already noted, some twelve years previous to *What's the point of it all?*, Damian had published his book *To grow in Christ: A plan for prayer*, the Foreword to which says:

> This "plan for prayer" is offered to you. Its purpose is easy to state: to enable you to grow in faith, hope and love by helping you to develop a richer, more personal life."

This little book is inspiring both in its simplicity and in its practical unlocking of so many important passages from Scripture. Readers who have done Kintbury sessions, especially a "Yes Week", recognise at once many elements which have evolved beyond the sequence of the standard exercises of the 3 day Kintbury experience. Damian the communicator had a particular appreciation for some of the outstanding Scriptural translations (and at times paraphrases) used by Alan Dale in *Winding Quest* and by Peter de Rosa in his *A Bible Prayer Book for Today*. Far from being any kind of dilution of the text, many of the passages from the Psalms and from the Old and New Testament have an immediacy about them which communicates instantly. It is good to see that many of these texts are to be found again in the encyclopedic *Walk in my Presence* brought to fruition by Brother Nicholas Hutchinson, Damian's faithful and talented amanuensis over so many years.

Given that this book began as a Lenten book leading to the celebration of the Easter mysteries, it is revealing to note the five titles which precede the Stage Six *Dying and Rising*: *Beginning, Listening, Remembering, Becoming and Sharing.*

Damian's own account of the beginnings and development of the Kintbury Centre pick up each of these same words, not necessarily with the same emphases, but with a consistency which underlines once again his passionate belief in what he calls a *work-in-progress* approach to the development of faith in young people and in adults.

Seven of the eight chapters of *What's the point of it all?* have a Kintbury context. But it may come as a surprise to many that Damian's work as director of the Kintbury Centre lasted only seven years from 1975 to 1982. It is true that he returned to direct many subsequent sessions at Kintbury but these were usually different forms of adult education of various kinds. The scope and variety of these sessions at national and international level is worth noting because it shows just how highly he was appreciated as teacher and communicator. This is far from being a complete list of Damian's many services to thousands of people:

* the Loughborough Summer Schools in religious education;
* the Newman College School which introduced James W. Fowler to Britain;
* Kintbury Schools of various kinds with Hubert Richards, Edmund Flood, David Konstant, Gerard Rummery, Herman Lombaerts...;
* the development of the LACE (Lasallian Association for Christian Education) seminars;
* his workshops, too many to be detailed, for many

different dioceses, Westminster, Nottingham, Shrewsbury, Manchester...;
* his "Baker Day" seminars (too many to specify as he left no day by day records) in many different schools throughout the country;
* his three visits to Australia and New Zealand for catechetical and religious life workshops;
* his visits in Asia, especially to Singapore, Sri Lanka, India, Pakistan as retreat giver and as leader of catechetical seminars;
* his many different seminars and retreats in Ireland;
* his work with his own Brothers in South Africa;
* his association with the Plano Retreat Center (Illinois) and his retreat for his Brothers from the Chicago Province;
* his many presentations on religious life or his experience with young people in the Lasallian International Centre in Rome;
* his membership of the International Catechetical Commission of his Institute (1978–1981);
* his highly appreciated contribution as a member of the Rule Commission of his Institute (1984–1985);
* his work on the National Project.

Damian's other writings

Damian's principal writings, other than the three books already mentioned, are his doctoral thesis treated elsewhere and his contribution to the *festschrift* in honour of Christiane Brusselmans, entitled *A Vision for Catechesis in the 1990's*. This is a carefully crafted essay written out of the richness of his doctoral research. It shows historical breadth and a deep understanding of the fundamental relationship between faith and culture. He faces courageously and with great clarity the question of the underlying conflict which has marked the catechetical movement since the second World War. Indeed, he finishes his article by asking in the first of the three questions which he felt arise from the analysis which he has presented, why catechesis should continue to provoke so much controversy, something which, as we know, caused him much personal stress during his work with the National Project.

The following tribute to Damian at the funeral Mass in Littlemore given by Brother Joseph Hendron, Provincial and long time fellow-worker with Damian in Kintbury, sums up many of the things which not only merited Damian the titles of *Communicator, Teacher, Writer…* but shows the essential link between these different activities:

> Many messages of sympathy that we received since his death make mention of the number of lives influenced, directly or indirectly, by Damian. And this is true. Our Founder wrote that the task of the Brother is "to touch hearts." More important than touching lives, Damian "touched hearts". He would not have been too inquiring as to the number of people who had heard of him, but he would have been concerned if hearts had not been moved to respond to God and neighbour by his person and his work. They were so touched, and he lived out the teaching of St. John Baptist de La Salle and the vocation of a Brother to the full.

Much has been made of the fact that Damian was a De La Salle Brother, though little has been said as to what this might mean. The official title of this group is The Brothers of the Christian Schools and it was founded in 1680 by St John Baptist de la Salle, a French priest trained at St Sulpice. De La Salle became involved in the education of poor boys and his meeting them changed his life. From being rich, heading for elevation in the Church (he was a Canon of Rheims cathedral at the age of sixteen), cut off by the very stratified nature of French society, he gave up his house, career and personal fortune to live with a group of teachers whom he trained. They eventually became "Brothers of the Christian Schools" for they saw this as the only way they could be totally dedicated to what was then a difficult task and to develop the personal skills and spirituality to do this as a gospel ministry. Over a forty year period De La Salle and the Brothers developed a spirituality suited to their way of life (community based and school oriented) and a methodology that enabled them to run good schools.

The fundamental spirit of the group was summed up in their desire "to be brothers to each other and elder brothers to the pupils". Their life was founded on the Spirit of Faith, a major inspiration being the story of the magi and their following the star (of faith) to the Christ child. It was in each pupil that, ignoring the outside, the appearance, faith enabled Christ to be seen in the poorest and roughest. The Spirit of Faith was founded on a love of Scripture, a personal knowledge of Jesus ("Do you know the person of Jesus as intimately as the Gospel writers?") enriched by personal and community prayer and inspired by a desire to remain constantly in God's presence. This led naturally to a Spirit of Zeal in ministry, for De La Salle saw education as ministry: "God has chosen you to make him known to others" and the pupils were to become disciples of the teacher who would model to them the Christian virtues.

By the time De La Salle died he had 100 Brothers. Today there are 6,000 Brothers in 84 different countries, working in partnership with 50,000 teachers. The changes in the Church since the Second Vatican Council have meant a greater sharing of the Spirit of Faith and a collaborative ministry which brings the richness of the whole Church community into education. Damian, in all his many ways, was actively engaged in and fully committed to this sharing of De La Salle, the Patron Saint of Teachers and all those involved in the education of the young.

4 | The Creation and Development of St Cassian's Centre, Kintbury

Kintbury was such an important part of Damian's life (as a Junior novice, as a teacher and then as the founder of the Pastoral Centre), that it was in many ways the geographical centre of his life.

We are privileged to have a very complete account, written by Damian himself for his Institute's series called *Lasalliana*, of the original vision which he had for this new Centre and of the various ways in which it grew into the Kintbury which continues to attract so many thousands of people today.

Before listening to Damian's mature reflections written some ten years after Kintbury had established itself as a Pastoral and Retreat Centre, it is interesting to hear some personal recollections of the early days from Brothers Dominic Green and Joseph Hendron, who were co-founders of the new Kintbury, as well as from Damian himself.

Damian had become dissatisfied with the spiritual development available in a school context and was searching for new ways to respond to the obvious spiritual hunger of young people. He was convinced that many sixth formers would be open to religious questions if these were raised in a less formal and more personal setting. He also felt that religious education could succeed only if it started from the doubts and questions with which the young people were filled but which almost all were reluctant to raise and discuss in a school setting.

Damian, the youngest of the three Brothers, was to be in charge, and together they were expected to launch something which was quite different from their experience. Dominic reminds us of the general uncertainty which marked the launching of this new project:

> Damian… was dreaming a dream. His hope was to establish a new apostolate i.e. a retreat centre for young people. It did not receive a 100% backing from the District Chapter (the periodic assembly of elected Brothers which determines policy) but rather a cautious acceptance of a trial period. Joe and myself were invited to join Damian in this new venture. I have to say in all honesty that, initially, Damian's 'dream' was a positive 'nightmare' for me, personally. I thought he was creating a monster. One of the reasons for the success of the venture, it seems to me, lay in the fact that the three of us were highly regarded as teachers, and coming from that professional background which was continued by the Brothers who followed us, proved to be an asset for a new venture. But we had to live with the uncertainty of the future and with what amounted to a suspicion on the part of some Brothers as to what exactly these three men were up to, especially as at that time we could more easily have been returned to the 'chalk-face'!

Joe recalls his own apprehension as well when that first group arrived. Good and experienced as he was in mathematics and physics, he was not quite sure on what ground he was expected to meet these incoming students. From the very beginning, some of the first groups included girls as well as boys, and the Brothers had little experience of working with girls. He mentions some practical difficulties:

> The arrival of students from outside required several adjustments to the style of life that existed when the Junior Novices occupied the building. The latter lived a structured life: caring for the house, washing up, regular prayer life, regular times for rising and retiring… I needed time to adjust to the presence of school students who had few of the domestic skills or general attitudes of the Juniors. Doing wash-ups after meals or making beds before leaving at the end of the retreat or

respecting boundaries (of the resident community) within or outside the house had all to be dealt with each time a new group arrived. Damian was tolerant in face of the new needs and, in fact, when one became used to it, explaining and insisting on the house regulations became an integral part of the retreat experience.

I can't recall how long the first retreats lasted but I think that quite quickly we settled into three-night formulas – arrive Thursday, depart Sunday or arrive Monday, depart Thursday. ...Looking back on it now, this programme just seemed to evolve. There was no blueprint initially. Damian had the skill to let it evolve and to be at ease in the middle of what seemed to be at times an unfocused process.

Indeed, the "unfocused process" sometimes forgot to take into account that with one group departing on Thursday and another one arriving on the same day, there was often no time for the hard-pressed team to slow down before the next group arrived. The pioneers insist that on one never-to-be-forgotten occasion they were still outside waving off the departing group when the succeeding group arrived! And at that stage there were only the three Brothers in the team! At least, this was useful in winning over the Brothers who were not quite sure of what was going on at Kintbury for, as Joe recalls, "Students from our own schools did some good propaganda work when they went back home: they reassured the Brothers there that the three Brothers in Kintbury were usefully occupied."

The early community and friends, especially Gus and Herman, did much work, redecorating, putting up partitions, making the Conference Room out of a big dormitory, designing the "shop", carting and carrying furniture, beds, cupboards, resources. It was typical pioneering. Gus continues to keep the grounds in pristine condition for the enjoyment of all; Herman has gone to his rest and is comfortable in Inglewood cemetery. Many a retreatant ate of the produce from Herman's market garden. With Herman there was no distinction between man, woman, child, volunteer or member of the order. If you were available he found a job for you!

The first retreat group with Paul McAuley arrived on a Friday evening in September 1975; as they disembarked from their minibus, Damian and Dominic left off painting the tea room at the top of the stairs to greet them!

And so St Cassian's began, informal, creative, imaginative; the first of its kind. The approach was simple enough on the outside: to deepen the faith of those who had it and to win to the faith those who hadn't. And how: *by bringing the Gospel message to young people without boring the pants off them, and by being willing to share with them: to listen, talk, pray, discuss and try to live the Gospel message.* Jesus invites (echoed later in God invites) how about listening?

There's nothing like good witnesses, especially outsiders, to change perceptions and what convinced the doubters that St Cassian's would be a success was the retreatants themselves. After the trial period, a working party was set up to assess and recommend. There was some significant enlightenment in the terms of reference:

> to research and co-ordinate the opinions of those who have used the Centre over three years; to evaluate the apostolic work being done at St Cassian's; to examine the property and adaptations which may prove necessary; to look to the value the District might place on the Centre in terms of financial commitments, personnel, etc.; to report to the Chapter in the light of its findings.

The working party came to this conclusion:

> This work appears to us to be blessed by God as a particularly useful contribution to the Christian education of the young. It is clearly in line with the guidance and practice of the Institute at large... The number of young people influenced by the Team is far in excess of the numbers they might be in contact with in school. There is a remarkable consensus – almost unanimity – of opinion regarding the good that is being done, the need to continue it and the improvements needed in the plant, emanating from the responses to the questionnaires... We were convinced this is a work we should be doing... We are impressed

by the Team's zeal and their effective charisms, but we are concerned that they may be overworked, that there is at present no provision to prepare others to carry on this work.

What had they discovered from their research? That the responses to the setting, homeliness and welcoming warmth of the place and people were enthusiastically favourable. That the style of the retreat sessions for young people and the long and short-term effects of this experience were always positive. In so far as these responses reflected the effects on the young people they are emphatic that they were beneficial; and most thought that the effects were lasting. Recommendations were made mainly in connection with accommodation, food preparation and community space, and major objections were also addressed.

After the working party had presented their report discussion ensued. It was clearly a "hot" issue because there were 48 recorded interventions! However, when push came to shove, the chapter voted 31 for, 3 against, to continue the Centre and to provide the personnel, finances and other resources for future development.

By this time, Damian had also become involved in the Loughborough Summer Schools for RE teachers and he hoped this would draw a broader clientele to St Cassian's than just De La Salle schools.

The pioneering nature of St Cassian's meant a change of life-style and approach. Initially the community was made up of De La Salle Brothers, but the non-stop pressure on such a small group and needs of the retreatants suggested something broader was needed, and the opportunity to offer peer ministry. The first advertisement for volunteers makes interesting reading:

The volunteers on that first team were: David Todd, Chris Higgins, Pat Donovan and Pat Wall. The success of the venture led Damian to see the importance of balancing the team with two young women. Bernadette Kelly and Nicky Francioni were the first of the feminine presence which has since been an important aspect of Kintbury teams. During a Yes Week, Nicky had challenged Damian on why there were no girls on the team and Damian was quite adamant it would not work and would cause problems. Nicky hinted that to have such a challenge was not necessarily a bad thing. She was one of the first to take it up.

The community currently numbers fifteen: seven Brothers, two Sisters and six volunteers and it attempts to live an integrated life for ministry and support.

Dominic muses over these first tumultuous years and remembers just what this Kintbury experience meant to him personally:

> I came to realise that I was in that place with Damian and Joe, and others who followed in later years, to help lead young people to Christ; to deepen the faith of those who had it and to win to the faith those who hadn't. We established the hallmark of Cassian's, which has continued for nearly twenty-five years – to bring the Gospel message to young people – to be honest and, hopefully, prudent in what we shared with them: to listen, to talk, to pray, to discuss and to try to live the Gospel message – not to dominate but to help. That was our ministry and all of this I learned from Damian who lived it!

In the light of these pioneering memories let Damian now speak for himself through the series of articles written in 1986 for his Institute's international publication, *Lasalliana*

ST CASSIAN'S CENTRE: TEN YEARS ON
A personal account by Damian Lundy

How was the centre brought into existence and why do people go there?

During the 1974 Chapter of the English Province of the De La Salle Brothers, I asked the Province to open a residential retreat-centre for young people. The Chapter had already decided to close our Juniorate (a boarding-school for boys aged thirteen to sixteen who were interested in joining the Brothers) and to set up a new team concerned with recruitment and the fostering of vocations, which meant that the large well-equipped country house in rural Berkshire where this pre-Novitiate formation had taken place was available. After the Chapter, I was invited by the Provincial (Bro. Victor) to join the new team, along with Bro. Joseph Hendron and Bro. Dominic Green. I agreed, on the understanding that the team's approach would include the establishment of a retreat-centre. This was accepted as an experiment for three years, beginning in the autumn of 1975. The experiment was to be assessed by the next District Chapter in 1978, with a view to the Centre becoming more established, if necessary in a different setting, or to its ceasing to exist, if the experiment had not been successful. It was also agreed that a financial subsidy would be assured by the Province. The new Centre was to offer to teenagers and young adults the experience of a residential retreat (though some misgivings were expressed about the use of that particular term), directed by the team of three Brothers with the participation of a chaplain, a priest who would either be invited to participate by the team, or who would accompany a group with whom he was already in contact (e.g. a local priest or a school-chaplain).

As Head of Religious Education at the Brothers' school in St Helens, from 1970 to 1975, I had joined with another of our schools in organising Young Christian Student (YCS) activities, which had involved a few residential visits. On certain occasions during the summer, St Cassian's had been used for these retreat-holidays, which had proved successful and popular with those taking part. I had become convinced that many sixth-formers who appeared to be so bored during Religious Education lessons would be open to religious questions if these were raised in a less formal and more personal setting, such as at St Cassian's. My experience with groups at Kintbury and elsewhere led me to this conviction. I also felt that Religious Education could succeed only if it started from the doubts and questions with which the young people were filled, but which almost all were reluctant to raise and discuss in a school-setting. Surveys and informal discussions confirmed my impressions.

The need for a residential centre with a programme specially devised for the needs of young adults and teenagers was experienced more widely than among the sixth form boys and girls of St Helens and Salford. I saw it as a general need in the British Church, and one which was being met only partially and inadequately. I was sure that, given the chance to make contact with other schools, tertiary colleges and parishes, the centre would flourish.

The experience of creative liturgy, prayer and discussion in the relaxed and friendly atmosphere of a charming old country house would provide the young participants with that for which many of them thirsted but failed to experience in the local parishes or schools: the experience of a Christian community, in which questions could be asked and experiences offered, so that faith could grow. The option, made in freedom, to help to create such a community for a few days, would offer the young people an opportunity which they would normally not have, and for which compulsory Religious Education (however well taught) and compulsory attendance at church or at religious services in school were no substitute. The full participation of teachers interested enough to accompany the group, as well as of the retreat-team, would bring the young people into personal and informal contact with adults, most of them committed to Christianity while sympathetic to the difficulties and questions of the younger generation, and not free from questions themselves. There would also be the opportunity to meet other young people, since, right from the early days, it was envisaged that, if possible, the Centre would be used by people from more than one place, coming together to form a single group, in which both sexes would be welcome.

Finally, the challenge to continue the experience (and develop its implications) beyond the few days spent in the centre would be implicit, setting up more permanent local groups to meet in liturgy and prayer as well as for social reasons – groups which would evangelise their members and the world in which they moved; a concern much discussed in the mid-seventies at various levels of the Church. How did this tie in with the teams commitment to fostering vocations to the Brothers' way of life? I was convinced that the work of fostering vocations to the religious life and the priesthood could not be separated from the work of building Christian communities more generally, which included praying together and sharing experiences on the level of personal faith, even if this was a searching and uncertain faith. This would often include the need to reject some "hang-ups" and misconceptions, the result of negative experiences which seemed to haunt many of the young people like ghosts, and which, if not addressed, were a major obstacle to growth into a more mature and personal faith. If this was hard to achieve in a classroom setting, limited experience had shown how different the picture looked when seen from the setting of a residential centre, at a safe distance from home, school and parish (frequently associated with these "ghosts"). If the Brothers were to attract young men to join them, if God's call were ever to be heard as a personal call addressed in love to each one, young people must taste what a Christian community could be like and what it could mean to celebrate the Eucharist outside a formal church setting, using music and texts to which they could respond as a group and as individuals. They must learn to relate to one another in faith and freedom, including a sharing of their questions and uncertainties. As they discovered their needs, personal ministry would be supplied by the retreat team and by the young people themselves, since a group which contains needs also contains gifts to cater for those needs. The work was fundamentally a work of evangelisation. I am writing this with the benefit of hindsight: it and its implications were to become much clearer as the team worked together during the early years, and as the numbers of young people coming to Kintbury grew considerably – into hundreds and then up to some three thousand each year, a situation which led to various changes in the facilities at St Cassian's, the structure of the programme and the size of the team.

What was the underlying theology behind the retreat-work at St Cassian's?

The basic conviction around which what quickly became known as "the Kintbury experience" was built is that each person has inherent value which is to be sustained and used (once it has been discovered) in the relationships which each one forms. A lot of teenage (and adult) "hang-ups" arise from the fact that, as people grow up, they acquire many negative self-impressions and they become blind to the good in themselves. However well-intentioned, parents and schools play a leading part in this situation. Often religion plays a decisive part in the process (so that it becomes a real enemy of faith), since the image of God with which so many people are encumbered is a basically negative and fearful one, which does nothing to help them grow, since they have no desire to relate with a God who is "like a merciless tyrant". Often a good deal of remedial reflection and action is required since a repudiation of "the God I don't believe in" may well be necessary before a search for an alternative God can really begin. This is not a private task, for we all need help and support, including affirmation to combat the self-depreciation which so many people practise.

My visit to retreat-centres in Australia and the U.S.A. in 1977 helped me to work out more explicitly what we had been trying to do in our centre since the retreats began. In Melbourne, a priest friend drew my attention to a slogan which, with some modification, was eventually to become a kind of motto for Kintbury. I express it here using my own name, as it needs to be personalised:

I'm Damian and I'm O.K
'cos God doesn't make junk, but he collects it!

The last four words were added by me, since though the first page of the Bible makes it clear that "God doesn't make junk – "God saw all that he had made, and indeed it was very good", two pages later on, the problem arises, told in the story of the Fall. (One recalls Karl Barth's answer to a fundamental-ist student who asked him if he believed that the Serpent really spoke. Barth replied, "I don't believe the Serpent spoke, but I believe in what he said!"). We note that God's judgement has traditionally been understood to include the first promise of eventual redemption. Throughout the developing revela-tion of God, as recorded in the Bible, people come to understand that, even if we make junk for ourselves and others, and turn the world in which we live into a junkyard, our dark human situation is relieved by the promise of God's salvation or healing presence for all who will accept him. We Christians be-lieve this was fulfilled in Jesus, the Lamb of God who collects the "junk" of the world (cf. John 1:29) not to use it against us as evidence of guilty complicity in that destructive process, but to offer us the hope of a more abundant life. (John 10:10).

This is the Good News we all need to hear at every stage in life, but nowhere more urgently and more comfortingly than in adolescence, with all its bewilderment:

> "that toil of growing up;
> The ignominy of boyhood, the distress
> Of boyhood changing into man;
> The unfinished man and his pain
> Brought face to face with his own clumsiness"

The challenge of the slogan ("I'm Damian," etc) is to let it question me and to respond to it honestly, to confront the reality in my life, and then, as a next step, to try to account for the reality by sharing my experience with others. I used to suggest that one could respond to the statement in one of five ways: by placing next to it a tick ("Yes, it's true!"), or a cross ("No, I don't believe it!"), or a question-mark ("I don't know"), or a tick and a question-mark ("Yes, BUT..."), or a cross and a question-mark ("No, BUT..."). As you will guess, the three responses which were most common were those which included one of the three question-marks, which signified an underlying question or series of questions, to be pondered and identified, alone and in a "sharing-group".

The team's growing experience of what we were now calling "ministry" led us to see that the work of healing had a key place in the retreat-experience, and that the implications of this meant that individuals were called to respond to the new life received by sharing it with others. It was in the United States in 1977 that I first heard and came to adopt the expression, "Become Good News!". This was another way of expressing the challenge implicit in another expression we often used at the time: "Kintbury begins when you leave!".

Each person is invited to share his or her discovery in the world to which they return with something to give, namely themselves. Bro. Simon Ryan, who made a strong contribution to the Centre for a few months during Kintbury's second year (1976–77), used to express the effect for the individual by quoting the final stanza of the W.B. Yeats poem I have quoted:

> "I am content to follow to its source
> Every event in action or in thought;
> Measure the lot; forgive myself the lot!

When such as I cast out remorse
So great a sweetness flows into the breast
We must laugh and we must sing,
We are blest by everything,
Everything we look upon is blest".

This non-Christian poem shows clearly the connection between self-acceptance, self-forgiveness and the singing or celebration of the resulting "sweetness" with which the individual is "blest". In Christian terms, it is God who forgives and accepts, when he is accepted; he is to be thanked and praised in personal prayer and in the liturgy of the group. It might be added that, from the very beginning, music played a big part in Kintbury. As well as praising God, it helps to build up and express a sense of community, so it was natural that it should punctuate the day and colour the style of liturgy, which was devised to allow individuals and the constituent groups to which they belonged maximum participation. Music and celebration are a natural response to God's generosity, discovered as an experience of the Good News: "It is by grace that you have been saved, through faith; not by anything of your own, but by a gift from God; not by anything you have done, so that nobody can claim the credit. We are God's work of art, created in Christ Jesus, to live the good life as from the beginning he had meant us to live it", is the Jerusalem Bible's attractive way of expressing Ephesians 2, 8–10. There are two connected responses: to sing the Good News, and to live it. The response will never be secured once and for all, for it is essentially a personal response to be made in the changing circumstances of life as well as expressed in the liturgy.

For the first couple of years, the sessions were less structured than they eventually became, and included a few elements which we later discarded. I'll omit the details here. Called to formulate the theology of the Centre to describe the process for a team which eventually came to include a few new members each year, I used to talk in term of the four *Becomes:* 1. *Become* **relaxed.** 2. *Become* **aware.** 3. *Become* **reconciled.** 4. *Become* **Good news.** In a few paragraphs which will not do justice to the variety of ways of opening up this pattern I will try to show its internal logic of how one *become* leads to the next.

1. Become relaxed

The first task facing the team meeting a group of young people, coming to the centre from two or three different places, is to help the newly forming group to relax together. Fear, nervousness, self-consciousness and shyness are of course common, especially on a first visit to the centre, and the work of the first evening must be to overcome these barriers which affect not only individuals in various degrees but the whole group. That means meeting in a big circle, after the evening meal, and introducing ourselves to the whole group – a painful business for many. The team tries to lead the way by offering models which the young people can use to talk briefly about themselves, their family, their special interests, and so on. Often a question, directly related to the main theme of the retreat, may be included, for instance "Can you remember ever getting lost or feeling lost when you were a child?" or "When you look back over the past few months, can you identify a high point and a low point?"

A few practical instructions and rules about the centre will follow, including such essential points as "no smoking in the bedrooms", "no disturbance at night", etc. Then there is a chance to continue the discussion informally mingling with new people before the evening ends with a night prayer. After singing some modern hymns (the participation being a good indicator of how relaxed the group has become!) and a couple of short readings and reflections, we would usually sit in darkness and pass round a lighted candle, each person being invited to make a short prayer before passing the candle to their neighbour. Prayers might range from "Please help my mum to get better from her sickness!" to "Thank you, Lord, for bringing us here!" to "God, I don't know if I believe in you!" to a period of silence, which might be awkward and embarrassed or reverent. Some times the silence spoke louder than words. The leader in introducing the prayer must recommend honesty: Don't be afraid to be yourself! Of course it may take some people the whole of the three or four day period to become relaxed, but if they make that step eventually (and the whole atmosphere of the centre is geared towards helping them to do so) they will have made a truly significant step, even if it is only the first one in our series.

2. Become aware

The task of "becoming aware" occupies the next full day of the retreat programme. After an informal morning prayer on the theme of the retreat (including some suitable Scripture, music and guided reflection), a presentation of the theme chosen for this retreat is offered by the team: the person directing this programme may give a talk, perhaps illustrated by extracts, music or slides, and often including a worksheet to be completed by individuals and then discussed after a coffee-break in small "sharing-groups" of about eight people (led by members of the team) to which each one is assigned, and to which they will belong for the rest of the retreat. The presentation is designed to help individuals become aware of themselves, of other people in their lives, of God (insider or outsider?) and to write down some answers to share in the small groups.

Having become aware of myself and some others, I can now become aware of these other members of my group and how they see life, what problems they face and where they look to find solutions. As time goes on, these groups can develop an intimate atmosphere of personal trust. This is always the intention, and much will depend on how skillfully the group is led—on the leader's self-confidence and sensitivity, including the ability to talk and be silent at the appropriate times, to encourage the shy and the reticent, to control the talkative, to challenge those who are hiding behind masks, to respond to and influence the dynamic at work in the group, and to encourage relationships to develop and deepen. You lead by example, of course, so you must be ready to share something of your personal story, if you are to ask others to do so. At the same time you must learn when to respect silence and how to help others handle silence and become at ease with it. Members of the team learn this by practice and by imitation, and by the mutual encouragement they offer to one another. Some have a natural gift for it, and their personal qualities make them fine leaders.

The growth in awareness of self, of others, of God in my life, is celebrated in a lively evening Eucharist, the different parts of which have been prepared by each of the small groups. The chance to work creatively together (say, in choosing readings and music, in preparing a collage or a mime, or in devising a penitential rite or a thanksgiving rite) enriches the relationships within each small group (even if it's often hard work and is another test of the leader's skills!), and the whole group benefits from this by celebrating a liturgy which is usually enjoyable, prayerful and lengthy (though the time is not usually noticed by the youngsters until the Eucharist is over). Exclamations of delight and surprise follow this unexpected success, which helps to consolidate further the life of this community which has existed for not much more than twenty-four hours, but which has been moving forward together—almost always at a rate and in a direction the young people had never dreamed of. We have just celebrated one of the communal and individual highlights of our life together.

3. Become reconciled

It is to be hoped that the movement of the group has brought its members to the third stage, where the challenge is to "become reconciled". The increased self-awareness of the previous stage normally includes some sense of what is incomplete, unhappy, inconsistent, unhealed or wrong in my life. "Things go better with peace", so how do I find peace? How do I become reconciled? A considerable part of the next morning will be spent facing this challenge as an individual, but the whole group and then the small groups must explore the need for reconciliation and the various ways of seeking this. Each one will be helped to prepare a personal programme for a quiet period (of about one and a half hours), which might include a period of personal prayer and reflection outside in the gardens and woodland or in the attic prayer-room, where the Blessed Sacrament will be exposed. Selected portions of Scripture and personal experience, and sometimes creative writing (e.g. a letter), might help. There may be an opportunity to go for an "Emmaus walk" with one other member of my group, with whom I choose to share more deeply my story and my problems; or perhaps the chance to have a chat with any member of the retreat-team I choose; or the opportunity to book a slot with the retreat chaplain for a personal experience of the Sacrament of Reconciliation. This latter opportunity became an increasingly popular feature of the retreat, as the centre developed. It is a sensitive and delicate area, and its success depends largely on the help of a sympathetic priest with whom the young person can relate and can trust. This is far more important than the mechanics of the Sacrament, though these may need to be explained and simplified to help and encourage those who fear this often unfamiliar and abandoned territory, which, if I can become sufficiently relaxed, may open up for me an unknown country which turns out to be the land of the Lord's healing and liberating love.

Very occasionally, friends might want to celebrate the sacrament together; more rarely a young person might want to invite a non-clerical member of the team to accompany them a very touching invitation, which I have experienced. For me, the theological model of the Sacrament of Reconciliation is to be found in John 21, where around the charcoal fire, Peter's symbol of failure and denial (See John 19, 15–18, 25–27), Jesus offers a new start to his friend, whom he calls by the name which recalls their first meeting (cf., John 1, 42) and to whom he gives another chance to say a threefold Yes, in love and friendship which will take the relationship beyond that threefold denial, as well as healing it (John 21: 15–17). The conversation makes Peter "saddened" or "deeply moved" (verse 17), but this is a positive experience which ends with a new call to "follow me" and undertake a dangerous journey where he "would rather not go", an inevitable feature of his commitment to be a good shepherd of Jesus's lambs and sheep. The consequence of this third step may well be the difficult task of going home and making peace, perhaps with a member of the family with whom ones relationship has become sour or empty, and which Jesus wishes to heal.

4. Become good news

To try building up such a relationship is a good example of taking the fourth step – to "become good news", a step which follows the retreat and which is the main challenge of re-entry into the familiar world, which will not have understood my retreat-journey. The experience is, after all, not a "one-off experience", but an invitation to understand that this opportunity has been given to me so that it can be shared. The sharing starts at home and in school, in my place of work, among my circle of friends and acquaintances, wherever I belong. First I may need to hear some explicit good news about myself, and this will be the purpose of the evening activity in the small groups, which follows a Eucharist on the theme of Reconciliation, designed to offer a communal opportunity to acknowledge our guilt and ask for forgiveness. This second Eucharist of the retreat is a rather quieter experience than last night's, but, instead of helping to prepare the liturgy, each person will be invited to participate by responding simply and personally at key moments of the Eucharist which will draw on their personal experience of the third step, around which the day has been centred. There is no room here to present a detailed description.

For many participants, the affirmation experience of hearing good news about oneself turns out to be the most powerful experience of the whole retreat. Before the small groups are resumed, the leader explains the point of the forthcoming session to everyone and tries to create a suitable atmosphere. A rather theatrical but highly effective method I often used was one I picked up from Australia. I would start with a blank sheet of white A4 paper and tell the circle, "Imagine this is you, at 7.00 am!" Then I would take them through a typical day, starting with a parental call ("How many more times do I have to tell you to get up? You should go to bed earlier. And look at the state of your room! It's a disgrace.") and quoting remarks from other members of the family, teachers, schoolmates or workmates, and so on – which amounts to a constant chorus of criticism and depreciation. For each comment, I would tear off a small piece of the paper and drop it on the floor, until by the time the character whose day I was describing had ended up in bed, I had nothing left in my hand except a tiny corner of the once beautiful and complete page. And from where I stood, surrounded by "junk", I would remind the audience (who had been howling with laughter and recognition of the familiar situation) that when others fail to run us down we are accustomed to take on the role for ourselves, helping the destructive process by which we get torn to shreds each day by the hurtful criticism which we have been taught to level against ourselves. And holding up the little corner of paper left in my hand, I would quote St Bernard: "Man is become like nothing, brought to nothing.

Indeed he is nothing... But how can he be nothing when God makes so much of him? How can he be nothing, on whom God's heart is set? If we are nothing in our own hearts, there is another opinion of us hidden in the heart of God."

The groups would then be sent off to help their members discover that "other opinion" hidden in God's heart. Called to be God's voices, we would tell each member of our group what we liked or appreciated about them, what we felt to be their gifts or positive qualities. There were only three rules: one, that of honesty – it was essential that the exercise did not become insincere flattery; two, that the appreciative comment must not be qualified, or the entire effect would be destroyed ("You have been very patient with me... most of the time!"); three, that the positive compliment must be accepted by the recipient and not denied ("Oh, but you don't really know me!"). To start this conversation may not be easy – another task for the leader's skills! – but once the youngsters start to lose their inhibitions and embarrassment, the effects can be extraordinary: tears of delight, broad smiles... When everyone has been complimented, the second half of the exercise begins. Each one thanks the group for the good news and is then allowed to speak briefly about one area in their lives with which they are dissatisfied ("I'm lazy", "I don't get on with my younger brother", "I don't like such and such a person", "I'm very shy", etc). The group then prays with that person individually and aloud, asking the Lord to help them resolve the problem, heal the suffering and show a way forward. The experience of ministering to one another's needs in this way (unfamiliar to most of those who first take part in it) often proves to be a powerful and deep experience of Christian love, as it is described in 1 Corinthians 13.

The final morning of the retreat would involve all those who came from the same place meeting together to evaluate the retreat, discussing its high points, low points, values and challenges, and deciding in what way it had been good news. As a group, they would then be asked to work out one or two specific projects that they might apply to their situation at home, in school, in the parish or locality, with a view to sharing the good news. Each group would announce its intentions, plans and hopes (as "the Gospel according to so-and-so") in the course of the liturgy of the Word, during the final Eucharist – a liturgy of thanksgiving and looking to the future, before the final meal, preparations for departure and farewells, full (sometimes dangerously full) of tears and songs and promises, which marked the re-entry into the familiar world.

I have tried to describe how the retreats at St Cassian's developed a pattern, and style which seemed to work very effectively as an instrument for youth ministry. Although I left the Centre in 1982 to undertake further studies in theology, I know that things have continued to develop at St Cassian's, as new people have come to work in the team, bringing new insights and modifying the vision and techniques they have inherited, to suit changing circumstances. That is how it should be. It shows that the Centre is alive and growing. Here I want to conclude my account with information about two other aspects of youth ministry as it has been exercised by those associated with this Lasallian development in England.

Are the aspirations of the centre being realised? How can you tell?

When people ask if the aspirations of the Centre are being realised, obviously I cannot offer any objective way of judging that. No professionally-conducted survey has ever been made, but I can point to the hundreds of letters received by members of the team over the years, in which the young people who have visited the Centre express (often very movingly) their joy and gratitude at the difference it has made to their lives. From the early days, a constant question was whether the effect would be lasting, and obviously it would be foolish to generalise. Nevertheless from the number of Kintbury contacts who still write to me from time to time, and from the stories and bits of news I hear in various places, I have reason to believe that a high proportion of those who have experienced a retreat at St Cassian's have been permanently affected by it in a positive way, some quite spectacularly, especially those who came back to deepen and continue their search for the new life. At times it was necessary to discourage some from returning, and to point them away from the tendency to treat Kintbury as a kind of drug, suggesting an alternative future direction for their search and a more realistic approach. All shrines and retreat-centres tend to collect their share of "groupies" (as pop-singers and film stars do) and the team must act responsibly and charitably to help the people who develop an unhealthy fixation with the place. A small number of young people have been actually banned from returning to the centre. Of course, most of those who become friends of the centre eventually come to realise when the experience offered by Kintbury has served its purpose and look for other ministries to serve their present needs. Sadly these can be hard to find.

To illustrate the successful way in which Kintbury has helped those who have used the centre, I can mention three or four examples from recent correspondence with people who are now in their middle twenties. To avoid any possible embarrassment, I will change all the names (except for David's, whose letter prompted this account).

Jack, who is studying with a view to training for the priesthood after some years of setbacks and disappointments, including bad health, wrote to tell me of coming across one of my letters to him encouraging him to thank God for his personal gifts and not to waste these. I cannot recall writing the letter, but its effect, after some months of darkness, was to lead Jack into praying again. Let him speak for himself: "Through this new deep prayer I had begun, I found I was like a new born child, searching for answers to unasked questions. In the Book of Sirach, chapter 2, the words, 'Accept all that happens to you' struck very deep. I realised that he had not left me but rather had been supporting me; he left me to find him, my own way... I felt I had to let you know that I found my path in life. Whether I achieve the priesthood or not, my path is always with and for God".

Silvia first came to us as a young police-woman, shocked by the Brixton race-riots which she'd been called upon to police. In Kintbury, at a key moment, she experienced God's healing love very deeply and learned to pray more personally, a feature of her daily life to which she has remained faithful. Having left the police, she's now doing a two year programme of youth and community studies, which she finds very challenging as her tutor is a Marxist. She is searching for a vocation to which she is almost ready to commit herself. She writes very openly: "It's a funny feeling – I definitely feel I have some kind of vocation – but he's not letting me know yet – which is fine by me – I'm enjoying myself – perhaps it's to be a youth worker – something that I've always had my heart set on – so we shall see... I still blame you for getting me into all of this – so thank you – I always remember you during my prayers".

I have already spoken about David, in the fourth year of his education degree. He worked with us on the Kintbury team for a year, after leaving school (not a particularly easy year, either!). You'll recall that I'm answering his questions here, which have stimulated me to go back over the familiar territory and re-tell Kintbury's story. I think David will make a fine teacher, and I found the concluding paragraph of his letter very moving: "While we are on the subject of St Cassian's I suppose that it would be only right for me, once again, to thank you from the very depths of my being for the chances you gave me to help me to become alive! We must sit down one day and I'll tell you an interesting tale of a young man's growing awareness of the God not out and beyond him but at the centre of his being".

"Work-in-progress"

What interests me about all these examples is that they are extracts from a "work-in-progress". The search is not concluded and the young adults know they must keep moving. Is it unrealistic to see these examples as the tip of the iceberg? I don't think so, for I could quote many others. Let me offer one more, from Judy, in her final year as a student nurse, who received a great deal from Kintbury and came back to help us a few times with our summer programme. She writes: "I think of you often and remember with affection the time that I have spent at St Cassian's over the years. You and many others had a profound influence on me during those often troubled times. Thank you!"

To Jack, Silvia, David and Judy, what can I say in my turn but, "Thank you!" (the Eucharistic dimension of Kintbury memories and the letters in which these are expressed)? What they, like so many others, have taught me is that to accompany others in the way of faith is always as much a matter of receiving as of giving; and that where "two or three meet in my name, I shall be there with them" (Matthew 18:20) is a promise that we can know to be "a saying that you can rely on" (1 Timothy 3:1).

One way in which the centre has tried to deepen the initial response it evokes

This account would be incomplete without at least a cursory account of the summer programme of "Yes Weeks", five of which are organised each year between late June and mid-August at St Cassian's. I am delighted to say that the custom has spread to other centres, and even to other countries. They have been devised as a follow-up to the usual three to four days retreat and their origin lies in two events. The first was the wish expressed by a number of those who had been to St Cassian's during its first year to return for a week's reunion, open to anyone who had made a retreat before. The team organised a special programme for this group, and the following summer two such weeks were arranged, the number increasing year by year until the present total of five weeks each summer was fixed in 1980. This was when the Brothers were celebrating the Tercentenary of our foundation and were encouraged to look for some needs which we were not meeting and to respond creatively to them. For us at Kintbury it was an opportunity to revise the formula of these weeks (until then popularly known as "jamborees") and to redesign the experience, giving it a more positive and challenging spiritual character. As a name for these attempts to deepen the initial retreat experience, we hit upon the term, "Yes week". "YES" was an abbreviation for "Youth Encounter Sharing", although this was soon forgotten with the "YES" coming to mean its standard positive sense of openness and willingness to respond to the invitations and challenges provided by others and by God. The idea is beautiful ... expressed in 2 Corinthians, when Paul swears "by God's truth, there is no Yes and No about what we say to you. The Son of God, the Christ Jesus that we proclaimed among you... was never Yes and No: with him it was always Yes, and however many the promises God made, the Yes to them all is in him. That is why it is 'through him' that we answer Amen to the praise of God". (2 Cor. 1, 18–20).

The "Yes Weeks" attracted a significant number of tertiary level students and young workers or unemployed. They were designed to cater for the sixteen to twenty-six age-group, with the understanding that many taking part would have left school and would have chosen to come to St Cassian's as individuals or with small groups of friends. The weeks are a joyful experience but sometimes a difficult one, since they are intended to encourage further growth rather than to pander to a sort of re-living of the original Kintbury experience, as though this were some kind of drug to "get high" on. Each season of "Yes weeks" has been based on a theme, usually the exploration of a particular New Testament book:

1980: My Relationships: Yes to others, Yes to myself, Yes to God.
1981: St John's Gospel: deepening my Christian life.
1982: Colossians and Philemon: Paul's vision of life in Christ.
1983: The challenges of St Luke's Gospel.
1984: The sacraments in the Christian life.
1985: (projected) An exploration of Acts.

Facing the challenges which life presents

The study of the Scriptural texts follow imaginatively designed patterns, and though these are soundly based academically, to show that my religious education does not stop when I leave school behind but moves into a new phase for which each one must assume personal responsibility, the real point of the week is to face the challenges which life at home, at school or work, in college and in society generally offers the individual who is trying to live a mature Christian life. We need the help and support of our brothers and sisters as well as of Christ to grasp these challenges, and the "Yes Week" makes this available. This is not the time to go into details, but one aspect of the experience deserves special mention: the practice of devoting one twenty-four period in the middle of the week to examining the implications of the theme being explored for one's sexuality, especially in view of the choices which young adults face in our society. Obviously this is an important aspect of life which most who come to Kintbury need to discuss, though usually the lack of time and the nature of the situation do not allow the topic to be opened up by groups during the standard retreats. Remember that the retreat-centre attracts young people from a wide variety of backgrounds and points of view (including many who are confused) and that the intention is to cater for sinners rather than for saints, so all can feel at home here (as they are at home in the gospels). I shall never forget the moment at the very beginning of an early "Yes week" when, during the introductory meeting, I asked for a volunteer to give an example of a personal problem or difficulty they wanted to face during the week, and an eighteen year old girl whom I shall call Kathleen announced immediately, "Well, my problem is very clear-cut: I'm in love with Mike, a married man who at this moment happens to be serving a prison sentence. Do I leave home and move in with him, when he comes out! I know how my parents will react". (So did I, since I had come to know her devoted and strictly Catholic parents!) The temptation is to overreact and speak out in a very condemnatory way, or to under react and fail to speak out at all. I have lost touch with Kathleen, but I do know that she eventually moved in with Mike, though fortunately she did not totally break relations with her disapproving and concerned parents. I think about her from time to time, and I pray that her life will be happy and that she will not lose touch with Christ, whatever becomes of her. For me, Kathleen was another invitation to stand beside so many anxious parents and educators and share their anxiety as well as their children's. Elsewhere I have called it "sharing the darkness". But to return to the "Yes Week", needless to say other members of the group were encouraged by Kathleen's willingness to share her problem so openly and frankly. She made it easier for them to share their own, and to keep a sense of perspective.

Another point about the "Yes Weeks" is that the team insist that the last twenty-four hour period of the week be dedicated to coming to terms with the practical implications of what one has discovered during the week in relation to everyday life, the context in which I live with my needs and my gifts and my choices. This may be a strong contrast with the Kintbury atmosphere of joyful personal support. Kintbury is not about escaping from life, but facing up to it. The danger for all retreat-centres, as I have said, is that they can become havens for those who are seeking refuge from realities which are too hard. The challenge is to show that God goes with us, goes before us indeed, inviting us to move forward. Marcos wrote from Chile (to which his family had eventually returned from political exile in London) to tell us that the memory of two visits to Kintbury was a continuing inspiration for him to try to do something about the desperate poverty in which some of his fellow countrymen were living and to try not to lose sight of God in the whole mess, because "life without the love of God is too hard".

After a "Yes week" in 1982, Jim wrote from South Wales about his efforts to work with friends to organise some lively youth liturgies in his own parish, of his continued praying over the topics discussed in the retreat, of further reading to deepen his own faith ("Now I'm in the middle of a fascinating book by Thomas à Kempis called Imitation of Christ…"), and of his discovery of the needs of his older spastic sister, whom he has taken for five walks in her wheel-chair: "I really thank God for that sister of mine and I really love her a lot". He goes on to reflect about the meaning of suffering in human life, especially in his own experience, to which Kintbury has opened his eyes.

A final point about the connection between centre and school. We have seen what the centre is about: opening eyes and broadening the vision. In my view, too often the education given in school seems to be about narrowing the vision; not in theory, of course, but that is the way it can work out. The pressures to conform (in terms of curriculum and pedagogical method) must be resisted, and the experience of a few days in a retreat-centre may offer a necessary Christian alternative, which could otherwise be lacking. In my view, the centre need not be too concerned about tying in with existing patterns in school-based RE. Let it concentrate on opening up a fresh vision and experience of what the Christian life is really about for those who choose to try it outside the organised sphere of classrooms, assembly-halls and so on, and, in opening up that vision to present a personal challenge to "choose life".

Afterword

Damian's own text certainly needs no gloss. Perhaps a fitting conclusion to his most personal appraisal of Kintbury (written upon request) after ten years is give some indication of how the Centre is flourishing now, and to remark that the publication of this biography coincides with the 25th anniversary of the founding of Kintbury as a Pastoral Centre. The mustard seed has indeed become a great tree.

By the 25th anniversary in September 2000, more than 60,000 young people will have "tasted" Kintbury; add to that the family weekends, the Yes Weeks and the LACE sessions and it is a huge number. Letters by the dozen, and these days e-mails galore, reveal the impact at a personal and group level. Many are the stories, many the life-changing experiences. There have been many tears and much laughter. Damian's and Gerard's book, *Growing into Faith* (1982) was in part inspired by their experience of people at Kintbury, as was Damian's *What's the Point of It All?* The pain of the world, experienced by the young, reveals itself there. The many folders from the Quiet Room speak of pain, bereavement, call, comfort, praise, doubt, hope, acceptance… the list is endless. For here young people feel able to reveal their inner selves, their hopes and fears.

A poem by W. J. Crockett sent to us by Sister Jo is poignant in its relevance to St Cassian's and the "Kintbury experience'.

A People Place

If this is not a place where tears are understood
Where do I go to cry?

If this is not a place where my spirit can take wing
Where do I go to fly?

If this is not a place where my questions can be asked
Where do I go to seek?

If this is not a place where feelings can be heard
Where do I go to speak?

If this is not a place where you'll accept me as I am
Where can I go to be?

If this is not a place where I can try to learn and grow
Where can I just be me?

It is a time of laughter, too, and social time and stories and games. Together, the Team and retreatants, forming community for a few days, offer support and ministry to friends, old and newly made. For seven years many experienced Damian first hand, and now by proxy.

For me, and for countless young people, Damian was Kintbury. His special gifts, charismatic personality, and genuine goodness made the experience of being at Kintbury one that literally changed their lives. He will live on, of course, in his songs which are now common currency in every parish in the country, and further than that. We have been richly blessed in him.

At one time he did fill the room with his size, but he always filled it with his bubbling, energetic presence, his zest for life, for all that lives, his marvellous ease with words and music, the colour of all he was and did. This life was too limiting for him – his gaze started here but always went beyond to what we could become, to what we really are.

Mark Dowle remembers his time on the Team:

I was there the second year without Damian Lundy and it was very noticeable that we were working in a team which did not have him. And people would arrive at the Centre and say "Where is he? We've heard about him". When he did come back he was incredibly supportive, but he didn't tie the success of the place to his name.

I was really surprised when I first met Damian. I know exactly where I met him; it was on the top of the stairs opposite the tea bar. He was coming down the stairs and I was going up the stairs and I said hello to him. There were people just changing session, that chaos that goes on, and I had to ask him something... but what struck me then and I remember very clearly. He focused on what I had to say and just phased out everything that was going on around him and we had this extraordinary two or 3 minute conversation. And I kept looking and thinking you're very ordinary. I expected you to be much more spectacular. Then I remember feeling genuinely listened to.

The Quiet Room is one of the most loved rooms in the house. Folders, going back more than fifteen years, contain prayers, reflections, hopes and fears. The retreatants leave them as a gift to those who follow; they also write their thoughts as an aid to reflection and intercession. Here are a few extracts that give something of the flavour of the contributions. They reflect pain, elation, insight, hope, doubt, trust, a sense of belonging, search. They are dipping into the well that Damian dug, they drink from waters that give life, a well that still runs deep.

When I arrived here I was frantic, tired and low. I was scared to be thrown into the boil with a load of people I didn't know. But as I settled in, I became calm, revitalised and suddenly very happy. I realised that God loves me, and I suppose that that's the wonder of Kintbury.

I hope you, too, find what you need.

Today, in my weariness, my sorrow and confusion, I came
seeking you.
Asking for a quiet heart, a peaceful mind, a gentle spirit,
Forgetting my trust in you, misunderstanding your love, too
much of a child to glimpse your purposes.
I was restless, unable to find my way into the stillness of the
moment, the beauty of that ever-changing now where you
reside.
Forgive me, Father.
This child's mind was too busy looking to see.

Seeing, hearing, knowing my distress, you came to me.
You came as the soft, shining early light and the fresh, clear air
of morning.
You came as the still, small centre of my broken thoughts.
You came as a conversation on a sun-warmed wall,
As the unexpectedly gentle hand extended in love
and the sudden revealing of a beautiful spirit.

This is your gift to me,
That I shall walk for a while in the darkness
That I may come to love the light more.

The cross is my comfort and my joy, at all times, in all needs.
I have come to see that when Jesus died on the cross it was not
an ending but a birth of something wonderful, the flowering
and fruition of God's love for his people. The love it expressed
has so many facets that new aspects of it will always be showing
themselves to me.
"Nails alone could not have held the God-man on the cross,
had not love held him there also."

I looked into the flame of the candle.
For some reason it resembled Faith.
It was quite small but it had a lot to offer.
So much warmth and light, which is needed for life.

Then in the molten wax I saw a reflection
This was my own faith.
Only a fraction of true faith,
it was very dim and so much cooler
Very often blurred,
almost disappearing but trying to hold on.

Lord I am only a reflection of you
but Please help me to become more like that flame
The flame of life.
Help me to shine out brightly
Share my warmth with everyone
And let them see you are so loving and
Essential to life.

Dear Lord

You know my indecisive nature – help me decide without hurting anyone. More than ever I am unsure of what love is, except in your case of course. Look after all those I really care about, those close friends sharing this Kintbury experience with me. I also pray for those I've met in Kintbury before.

Love you always – thank you for what has been, sorry for what hasn't been.

Through life we suffer in silence, our problems we bottle up. But here emotions are allowed to show whoever we are, wherever we are from. You and your helpers provide a loving harmony which permits us to think and face our problems either alone or with a friend.

Thanks Lord for Kintbury and the people here who have shown thought for me.

The experience of small groups, the making of new friends and the Emmaus Walks have generated lasting friendships and even the occasional marriage. One member of staff who returns regularly with school groups bore witness one evening to the wonderful fact that his Emmaus Walk partner seventeen years ago is still a very good friend and they meet and communicate regularly. The creative thinking that led to the inclusion of young people on the Team has enhanced the ministry of Kintbury and transformed the lives of retreatants and team members. Kintbury is proud to maintain the tradition set down by Damian as a living thing, responding to current needs and offering a fresh range of retreat activities and experiences.

Damian loved socialising and for him the relaxing time in the evening before night prayer was always a joy. It was a chance to exchange experiences. There were the stories and games, many of the former against himself for he could see the humour and irony in events and coincidences. A number of people have remarked on the impact this jovial, hearty, relaxed and generous man had on them.

One of the tiring aspects of Kintbury is night-time supervision, with the parallel male and female wings aggravating the experience for a willing but frustrated staff. On one occasion Damian was supervising, only to discover a cluster of lads at a window; they were obviously intrigued. Opposite was what David Attenborough would describe as "display behaviour". Off Damian stormed.

"YOU, get into bed!" He drew the curtains.

"I have a phobia about curtains," came the reply.

"We don't take people here with phobias," was an equally quick response.

Later the next day it was Affirmation time. The young woman was in Damian's group. He read on his page: "I likes you by day, but I don't like you by night!"

Affirmation time is the culmination of the retreat; not the last event but the central event. The whole process from welcome to awareness to celebration to Emmaus walk to Quiet Room to reconciliation heads this way, to a kind of Transfiguration experience which eventually leads to a descent from the mountain, back to the "real" world where the invitation is to be good news. What does an Affirmation evening tell us about how we treat each other in our everyday lives? About how we relate? About the pressures we put on each other? Damian was forever asking questions.

Many visitors to Kintbury know about the taxi driver, but it bears repeating. Imagine you are crossing London in a taxi heading for Paddington. The driver, with typical curiosity, asks "Where are you off to?"
"You wouldn't know. It's just a little village."
"Try me".
"We're going to Kintbury."
"You're not going to St Cassian's?"
At this point the driver opened the glove compartment and took out his worn, tattered, much-thumbed but clearly loved affirmation book. "My group gave me this many years ago on my stay in Kintbury. I treasure it dearly and read it often." Tingle factor or what?

I hope the picture I have painted reveals a jovial character, rich in God's gifts, sociable, full of fun, liking a pint, musical, joke-telling, consummate actor and mimic, and totally accepting. Warmth was his middle name. A memory from a regular visitor describes him thus:

> My mind is full of pictures of Damian from the first time I accompanied some sixth formers to Kintbury and met this amazing Tweedledum figure in an enormous OXFAM cardigan.

So what is your memory of Kintbury? A moment's pause, perhaps for that "emotion recollected in tranquillity" so beloved of Wordsworth and relevant here. The fire that Kintbury ignites has the ability to retain its heat and energy throughout a lifetime for the heart has been touched.

Damian, humble as ever, having set up the Centre eventually moved on. He did return for a variety of events and visits, including school retreats. It was touching to listen to his conversations with retreatants who would ask if he had been to Kintbury before. His deep chuckle would accompany his conspiratorial smile "A few times!" It was another example of giving the Centre its own life and vitality and not expecting it to be dependent on his name and reputation.

From time to time he would reduce his bulk. It was at Kintbury that Damian went through a number of re-sizing phases! The photo that accompanies his articles in *The Sower* casts doubt as to whether it is the same man. On one occasion he went to the doctor and was told to lose forty-nine pounds weight (before metrication!), and to take at the most one pint of beer a week (O attenuated Lent!). Some time later he met Vin as he was heading off to catch a train: "My case weighs forty-nine pounds," he said, "and that's how much weight I've lost!" No wonder Joan admired his celery-stick control. His dad was a Master Baker, superb in pastries and cakes, Vi, his step mum, was Yorkshire's finest cook and preserve maker, ever-experimenting with Beef olive, Rumpty Tumpty (her familiar term for delicious fresh fruit preserved in rum), apple pies with melt-in-the-mouth pastry, fish pies, Mediterranean salads... And from time to time they visited Kintbury to make sure the team was aware of such culinary specialities. So Damian was brought up to admire and enjoy the good gifts of God. He was a naturally comfortable character in whose presence it was easy to relax. It was surprising what questions he would slip in over a bit of late night toast. For him the image of the Kingdom as a marriage feast or a banquet was just right.

It made his subsequent illness harder to bear, for his kidney failure meant he could not eat most of the foods he loved, his

Damian at Cambridge

Louis Welker,
Damian Lundy, Rome 1979

The Malt House, Newent
Photograph of a painting by Maureen Carter 1986

Rome 1984

Damian, Christopher and Louisa at Worth

pint remained behind the bar and his glass of red wine became a memory. He knew he would have problems for he had inherited kidney cysts from his mum. From time to time one of them would swell and burst, causing him considerable pain and gradually increasing the size of his kidneys. He said that one day the surgeons would have to remove one of them because there would not be enough room for both.

In the midst of this inside knowledge he was able to radiate joy and laughter. No one would have known. Damian knew pain, he lived with threat; his writings have inbuilt prophecy and dramatic irony. He knew a little of what the plot would be. It made him so much more accessible to those in pain themselves. That is why the Kintbury experience relates so well and easily to those who suffer; it is integral to the breaking of bread, a recognition of brokenness. From here the living, healing waters flow.

5 | Damian's Gift of Friendship

Perhaps one of Damian's most remarkable gifts was his ability to make friends with so many different people. This was not simply a kind of veneer but something much deeper. He was genuinely interested in others and had the ability to be present to them in his own inimitable way. The variety of persons at Damian's funeral and the extraordinary number of written or telephoned tributes illustrate the vast world of his friendship. Family members, brothers of his own religious congregation, priest friends, professional colleagues, former pupils, so many persons who had been to Kintbury, nurses from the hospital, parishioners from Blackbird Leys where he, and members of his community, helped with the liturgy and sacramental preparation of some of the young people. He shared his friendship easily and he also shared his friends. He developed a special closeness to those with whom he lived, or worked or studied. He valued such friendships and many letters and some of his finest poetry were written at various times to those whose friendship meant so much to him. But there was never a limited group of insiders with Damian. Each one mattered, each one was valued. It is because of these wide ranging and deep friendships that we know so much about him.

Here is a particular example of Damian's concern for one such friend, Gerard Markland, one of his students in the Juniorate and Brother in temporary profession, just after he had decided to leave the Brothers and was facing up to a new school year in a new school:

> I do hope everything has gone well for you in recent weeks and that you are happy about your decision. I know you've gone through lots of uncertainty, but I imagine it was not easy to reach a decision when you did. Anyway, for what they are worth, I offer you my best wishes, prayers and sympathetic support, and I hope you'll be very happy indeed and quickly overcome any problems of adjustment. I hope too that we might continue the partnership we've enjoyed at odd intervals when working together on words and music. I think you have a real gift for composing good tunes, especially suited to those scriptural passages, in that they are sensitive and expressive, not too difficult to sing well, and they wear well too!... I end with a few lines of verse which I wrote for you last Easter and which I hesitated to send in case you might be embarrassed by having 'odes' addressed to you.

This letter deserves a few comments. The "few lines of verse" are, in fact, the remarkable poem given below. One senses as well that the hesitation on Damian's part – after all, he tells Gerard that he had written the poem last Easter and it is now September! – was his own sensitivity and a deep concern neither to influence nor preclude his friend's personal decision by sending him, just at this moment, the gift that this poem represents.

For Gerard
Easter 1977, Kintbury

Time plays strange familiar tunes for us
to dance to, their rhythms seasonal yet unpredictable
as summer, always releasing fresh emotions.
What was it Dylan Thomas wrote of Time?
"The green unraveller". That's true. Time plucks
at the strings, unstitching. I have kept counting
new holes, fresh rents, and separations, threads
hanging loosely, spaces spreading around each
island. Writers I've read, friends like you, supply images
of Time's music and undoing, and these have opened

my blinking eyes to people, events and other fragments
weaving, unweaving, a tapestry, ravelling, unravelling,
continuous as music, green as life. It's hard to take.
Now you have become a traveller, poised at a crossroad,
like a pilgrim set on a definite, separate journey.
Please pardon the valedictory tone! this poem was never
intended to be an elegy. It is a call to celebrate
fragmented sense and music drip into this cup,
my verse where I offer promises, prayers, memories,
each hesitation first calls, last
desperations, joys, certain anxieties and
uncertain hopes, each "Do not be afraid"... so, smile.
This drink has become a blessing-cup for you:
It's yours! It's wine. It's blood. Take it and drink it.
It is your past. Celebrate it in songs!
And to the future you accept, go forward
sailing proudly, not sadly, not sadly. Go singing! Play!
Strange familiar tunes for us to dance to.

Damian
Auckland, 11th September, 1977

Brother Thomas Campbell, who as Provincial had Damian as
one of his auxiliaries, and worked closely with him over many
years, writes of Damian in terms similar to so many others who
valued his friendship:

> With his rich giftedness, it is not surprising that Damian had
> a finger in many pies. He had that special gift of finding the
> right words to capture the sense of the debate and encapsulate
> it in a resolution that moved us forward when discussion was
> becoming tedious. The same gifts were at work in many of the
> Team meetings where we prepared for Staff Days or Community
> Visits... Even before launching the St. Cassian's project in 1975,
> Damian had established himself in catechetics and youth
> ministry when he taught in St. Helens... Working with him was
> a real education. He went on to co-write and co-edit a rich
> body of catechetical material. And, with others, he bore the
> brunt of criticism and misunderstanding. He was a great servant
> of the Church but retained a healthy and critical stance on so

many questions. You were rarely bored in Damian's company, but you were very often exhilarated, encouraged and frequently amused.

Brother Benet Conroy, who shared an office with Damian for four years, has his own fund of stories about what Damian called his ' biblical filing system', based mainly around the Gospel maxim of "Seek and you shall find." But Benet shared so much of Damian's last years as his chauffeur and co-worker that he writes of his friendship:

> Damian had become my best friend in the Institute and I shall miss him sorely. The community always had a "buzz" when Damian was around. He sparked off all kinds of exchanges, serious and humorous, and he could be a bit of a tease. After a demanding day's work he would love to sit and relax, telling story after story, able to muse on his misfortunes and laugh.
>
> In the past few years it was a privilege to work with him on the Provincial Team and to be part of many of the beautiful things he was committed to – his involvement at Sacred Heart, Blackbird Leys, the LACE weekends and the staff days in schools… He had such an attractive personality that everyone was drawn to him.
>
> I was so fortunate to have the chance to spend real quality time with him in Rhiw, North Wales, before I moved on from Oxford. We took huge volumes of dialysis fluid with us, and a determination to make the best of a magnificent week. We relaxed, visited, sat and soaked in the beauty. We were intrigued by the wholeness of Porthmeirion, enraptured by Snowdonia on a perfect summer's day, pleased to return in the evening to home-cooked food, often pasta. The Catholic Church in Pwhelli had a small, high-quality choir to support the singing, and Damian sat and listened to beautiful renderings of some of his works!
>
> It was the first chance Damian had had of a holiday for a long time. It also gave me the chance to spend time with him just before my move to Dublin. You can imagine how devastated I was to receive the news of his death. Just before he left for Rome we had spoken on the phone and arranged a date to meet in December to prepare the Children's Christmas Liturgy for Sacred Heart Church, Blackbird Leys.

Many people were asked for their memories of Damian, and if this happened face to face or on the phone, invariably they would break into laughter. Spontaneous, joyful, calling back to memory a meeting, a joke, a story, a dance, a song, a greeting, a hug. Groups of friends considering his impact on them might initially be serious, pensive, a little sad, but give them a minute or two and the laughter would break through like sun after showers. He had that effect.

From time to time he would send verses to his friends, as thank you tributes or as invitations. These range from the highly amusing to the seriously observant, but always grateful. Occasionally, friends who had helped him in some way were the recipients of one of his own poems.

We owe this very personal poem to the courtesy of Dorothy, who, through the De la Salle Brothers in Australia and at Brother Gerard Rummery's suggestion, came to work at Kintbury in 1980 as part of her *practicum* in Counselling with Reading University. Dorothy will be well remembered by participants in Kintbury Sessions of 1980–1981, especially during the "Yes Weeks," and by the Oxford Provincialate community for the wonderful Christmas dinner which she cooked, with Damian, in 1995. Typical of many religious houses, the kitchenware and cooking utensils were a motley collection from various other (closed) houses, and often the mix did not match. Dorothy (affectionately known as Dot) provided the community with a lovely set of pans as a goodbye gift. From then on they were known as the "Dot pots".

To appreciate Damian's own note accompanying the poem, the name given to Sister Dorothy when she first entered the convent was Sister Borromeo. As you will recall, the same type of name change happened to Damian when he joined the De La Salle Brothers: from Michael to Damian. Damian writes to Dorothy:

> I've been reading a glorious book by Prue Wilson (former Provincial of the Sacred Heart Sisters in England) called *My Father took me to the Circus: Religious Life from Within*. Well,

quite out of the blue, when I'd finished the first chapter I started thinking about you and got the inspiration for a short poem. I've tried before to write something for you, but nothing ever materialised. Well, here you are! Perhaps the first line means: "I was expecting Mother Borromeo, when in walked Sister Dorothy!"

For Dorothy

A nun, he said. His tone assumed an image
of veiled constricted passiveness in a cage.
Into my life you burst, caring like few others,
Raising those questions, caring ("Gently, Brothers!"),
And always provoking life – bracken uncurling
In the damp morning, as well as sparks whirling
From a night bonfire blazing up, rather than smoking;
Your smile, your words, your kindly presence poking
Me in the ribs with detailed questions,
And I stumbling to grade my answers into sections,
Lines which won't rhyme, or crazy midnight sessions
To solve the vast world's problems at St. Cassian's!
But let me say Amen to you, my love! Please know I thank you
For all you ever meant to me, mean now, and always will do.

What a delightfully translucent cameo, his own "eucharistic postcard" to a really close friend. In 1997 Dorothy was able to come to England with a group from her school in Australia, and she took the opportunity to visit Oxford and see Damian's grave. It was a moving occasion. She has retained an active and prayerful interest in Kintbury and follows its fortunes in the Newsletter. She and Benet communicate from time to time, and Damian is a common topic for consideration:

> It will be Damian's anniversary in ten days. It is still hard to believe he will not suddenly come into the room. His influence here is strong, and I'm trying to encourage him to take an active interest in the new things we are trying to promote. Incorporating them into our normal programme is going to mean some adjustment of mind and planning. It's all his fault since he wanted me to come here and try to move the place on!

The Dowle family, two of whose members contributed years of service in Kintbury teams (as did Nicky, wife of Mark), were the recipients of one of his very best poems, which is reproduced here with the consent of the family.

THE MALT HOUSE, NEWENT: JULY 1983

I remember a house
and a garden sunlit, heavy with fragrance
and filled with love
and children calling from a secret place
behind flowering shrubs
and a white rabbit munching contentedly
on lettuce, with a guinea pig, Rusty,

all shyness and softness
where old brick steps with a winding path
lead up to a lawn. Listen to the thud
of a croquet ball and the whoop of success
(or a groan!) here, where all is summer joy
on the warmest of days,
cold cider on the grass, contentment even in talk
of an absent brother a continent away, recalled
in the laughter of friends together.

I remember a house
filled with good time, good people: three brothers
big and generous, with their friend, and a serious little girl
with a decisive frown
presiding over a game; and Fred, a tortoise
as old as his master
but slow and wrinkled and laden (so you'd never
guess he was seven!);
a cat called George who boxes with people, then
flees into shadows from Brambles, springer
spaniel, storybook dog. Here, all
is alive, all interest and concern. And the young
man who into the night sings of his future
makes even bewilderment sweet,
when he fingers it into music through guitar strings,
lets it be shared as a song.

I remember a house
and a circle of friends outside on a summer night
around a half open door,
now that, upstairs, the little boy sleeping
in bed, surrounded by teddy bears, undisturbed
by the singing below,
dreams of Paddington Bear and jigsaw puzzles and spelling!
In the fading light on the garden's edge
friends have come together
to weave, from a moment of quiet, affection into
delicate, prayerful wishes –
and all the delights of the summer day gathered
into familiar tunes.
A band of music makers – and on they play
they never want it to end, this evening, this glowing
summer, this garden, this joy.
I remember a house
'Where love is, God is,' they say. I'm sure.
I taste it now and here he is found, the night
still heavy with perfume, the slow

day transmuted to memories, echoed in singing,
still lingering; here he is found in you,
my friends, his images;
a God who is gentle mother, caring for all,
so unobtrusive and all embracing;
who is father, provider, maker of gardens,
known in his gifts but loved
for himself, and for the love in which he is found
in song, in game, in garden, in family, in house –
all images of life, of friendship, of grace,
of all that is shared
by us all in this place tonight.

I remember a house;
and here on this ground, in this garden, –
I have stumbled upon an Eden.
I recognize it, precious and inexhaustible,
discerned in the colours of flowers and in their perfumes,
intensified in a single scarlet rose,
but scattered around also in soft white petals,

green in leaf and stem, blue in small bells, trailing in honeysuckle,
golden, spilling
over that old wall from another garden
into this living given abundance offered to all
the senses, caught in the music
of voices, reflected in shining eyes
in a circle where all are welcomed, an emblem
of peace, a renewing soil,
yes, for each person to grow.

I remember a house…
And the young man, Aidan, who into the night
sang of his hopes: he was Adam redeemed, he
had nothing to fear, but only a new
chance to decide, a call to discern,
ambitions to fulfil, time,
and a home to build like this for another family.
Keep playing! Your friends' eyes follow those agile fingers,
your parents, brothers and sister, listen, delighted.
Keep singing! Remember (children
are waiting!) there's ground
to be turned into fragrant garden.
Keep growing! You have, dear friend,
not only songs to compose, old dreams to keep exploring;
for an open gate leads to a waiting road,
yes, and a future for you to design.

Damian Lundy

With my love to Tessa, Julian, Gerard, Elizabeth, Christian, Aidan, Peter and Mark, and my thanks for an unforgettable weekend at the Malt House.

Damian himself wrote a letter giving explanations of the poem. It is worth offering it for consideration:

A note for friends:

It's not a good sign when poets issue notes to help their readers. I hope The Malt House reads well enough without notes, but in case you are curious let me tell you how the poem was written.

Aidan Dowle had written to me after his visits to St Cassian's Centre, Kintbury, where I had already met his parents. He invited me to spend a weekend with the family, and I accepted, after my university exams, during the first weekend of July 1983. I'd been working hard and needed a break. I also wanted to interview Aidan's dad, Julian, about his voluntary work for Catholic Youth in Gloucestershire.

And there was a further reason. Aidan wanted some advice about a decision he was faced with: should he accept the invitation, to go to Plano, Illinois, to work in a retreat centre there for a year?

We talked about this during a walk on Saturday afternoon. Saturday evening and most of Sunday were spent relaxing in the beautiful garden with other members of the family and various friends, including a small group who met for an evening of croquet together which ended with a short time of prayer and singing. The weather had been glorious. That evening time of reflection was quite magical. It ended indoors with Aidan singing some of his own songs, expressing something of his dilemma and sharing feelings of uncertainty. The poem alludes to this in verse 2, and Aidan is addressed personally in the final stanza.

Who are the Dowle family, to whom the poem is offered as a tribute?

Julian designs gardens – brilliantly. He won the Chelsea Flower Show's Gold Medal for his skill in this regard. This explains some of the poem's imagery and vocabulary, including the final verb of the last stanza.

After working in New Zealand, Julian and his wife, Tessa, moved with their family to the little rural town of Newent in Gloucestershire, where they bought the old Malt House in the High Street. They are still working on this lovely property, which they decided to make into their family home. The garden is every bit as delightful as you might expect. I hope you'll realise this from the poem.

Some of the allusions will not require explanation. I might mention the members of the family. Mark (21), Peter (19) and Aidan (18) are the three elder brothers of verse 2; their friend, Damian Stayne, was also a guest for the weekend – and also considering an important personal decision. Peter, in fact, was away but very much present in spirit, as was Christian (15), the "absent brother" of line 15, who was at an international scouts' camp in Canada – an absence which somehow pointed to Aidan's eventual decision to go to the States. The youngest children are Elizabeth (9) who presided carefully over the croquet, and Gerard (7) who is as delightful as the poem suggests.

Incidentally, the croquet set was a new acquisition, which not only gave us all great fun, but also harked back to the nostalgic setting of Edwardian books like *Peter Pan* and *Wind in the Willows*, part of my own childhood nostalgia and somehow appropriate to a time when a young man was facing a decision about whether to take leave of such a wonderful home and family.

The poem celebrates the values of home, family, childhood and Eden, while accepting the inevitability and desirability of moving out and moving on. I dedicate it with affection and gratitude to all the members of the Dowle family. I'll never forget that glorious weekend. I hope the poem (started on my way back to Manchester on Monday 4th July and finished on Boxing Day, 1983) will allow some of my friends to share the memory.

Damian Lundy
1 January 1984

Family recollections sixteen years later are fascinating!

I remember his weekend here very well. He was very tired and it was a very relaxed weekend. It was a very hot time, a lot of fun, very funny, nothing too heavy. Damian went out into the garden to read and went to sleep. He came down and said, "I never do that! I never just switch off and relax."

What doesn't come out in the poem was the cheating that was going on in the croquet. nine year old Gerard had his own special croquet mallet. It was almost as if the whole seriousness of life was bracketed for a day or so. Can anyone remember Stella Gibbons' *Cold Comfort Farm?* "There is nothing finer than England at 7 o'clock on a summer's evening." It was that kind of recreation.

I remember being very touched that he wrote the poem, that somebody thought that much of us.

In the poem he notices so much: 'Dreams of Paddington Bear, jigsaw puzzles, spelling.' That's interesting, he came as a visitor to the house and your (Gerard's) interest at the time was jigsaw puzzles and he's obviously spent time finding out about the youngest member of the family. It's not like he's just come to see the adults.

Another good friend to whom he wrote cheeky verses was Bernadette, who worked long hours and with very good humour in the National Project Office. She shared with Jim and Damian and Anne the delights of the balcony overlooking Cromwell Road and the Natural History Museum. She brought relief to what was often frustrating work, sometimes when he was quite ill or even dialysing. In return she was celebrated and greeted in verse. To her delight she offers the words to a wider readership.

Damian would bring visitors, occasionally Bishops, to the office to see different aspects of the work. There in her glory was Bernadette. Lively, outgoing, cheerful, hospitable, good fun, observer extraordinary. So what about the shoes, Bernadette? She gives the explanation, which takes place as part of a dialogue:

> **Bernadette**: He'd bring visitors round and say 'I'd like you to see this'. Under my desk I'd have all my different coloured shoes. I walked three and a half miles to work each day, you see, and then I wanted to change into something which went with the outfit I'd on. So I had all the different coloured shoes under there. And of course they all laughed. But he was terrible! The ones he liked best were my red ones.
>
> **Jim**: He wrote a poem about them.
> **Bernadette**: He did.
> **Benet**: More than one poem. I've got them.
> **Bernadette**: O great! I wore red a lot so I'd have red shoes on.

So here they are, often accompanied by an anonymous, cryptic note in very characteristic handwriting (especially the 'k'):

> O Sadie of the solemn face,
> Beware the pleasures summer brings,
> Lest these thy resolution wound

And tie thy virtuous feet in strings.
But lest thy resolution bold
Should strain and crack or show a chink,
Put on they scarlet shoes, O Maid,
Trip heavenward and take a drink!

Signed: An admirer

To Sadie Sprout, the divine Sprout!

O Guardian of the mystic hook,
Thy scarlet shoes had gone!
O prince's daughter, fairest nymph,
In radiant joy glow on!
Thy office still provides a frame
For every waif and stray.
Thanks for thy loving care, belov'd!
I'll come again some day.

Signed: Anonymous

He writes to his beloved:

Dear Sprouting, every word from you
Relieves the gloom of wintry days,
Sends beams of sunshine and of hope
Dispelling gloom with glorious rays.
Oh may we meet ere long, my dear.
I'll dialyse and you may cheer!

Love Damian

O prince's daughter in garments of gold (not to speak of the shoes!), thanks for your letter and autumnal card! Sorry it rained on you in Scotland.

I struggle onwards, still dialysing three times a week. Another (minor) operation to come on Monday next – to *improve* the dialysis (which is *not* working too well!).

You tell me to keep smiling, but how can I, when 'change and decay' is all around – and even the sprouts are withering on the stem!

Love Damian

The reference to the operation was for the insertion of an artificial graft made of gortex into his forearm to enable the dialysis needles to have somewhere to go and flow freely. Unfortunately the first one failed and the second one was ineffective. He had to resort to neck lines again.

> O Sadie, blooms thy love so sweet
> That from it shoots life giving power!
> With trembling hands I ope'd the seal:
> Within my hands a cheque did flower,
> Signed with fair Sadie's dearest love.
> Surprised, I saw (yea, saw with sighs)
> What else but treasure long forgot
> And thereupon resolv'd to spot
> A *tratoria* fine to prove,
> Dear Sadie, ever loving, wise,
> That distant days, recalled, are not
> To pass without we hail with love
> Remembered moments, friendship true,
> The times we laughed, the joys we knew.

> Beloved,
> the above sonnet is a posh way of inviting you to come to Oxford for a celebratory meal – a worthy way of spending some of the cash you sent. What a lovely surprise! We'll fix a date for the celebration on Thursday when I'll be at E.Sq. for CAXE, and will need a hoook!! Confident that you will supply one with lavish TLC!

The references above to 'hooks' meant he had changed to CAPD dialysis and needed something on which to suspend his litre bags of fluid.

Damian needed people who stretched him, and one notable friend did that with skill. So here is offered a consideration of a friend who must have been a champion for him. Each fired the other. As a model of friendship, that of Damian and Gerard was very strong, of almost biblical proportions.

Among Damian's closest friends for some twenty-seven years was Brother Gerard Rummery, an Australian, who arrived in England in 1969 to begin doctoral studies. For a little over two years, 1970–1972 and for some months in the summer of 1973, they were both members of the same community at St Helens while Gerard was working at Lancaster University or in Europe as he completed his studies and prepared his doctoral thesis.

They had first met briefly in January 1969 in the Brookside community at Cambridge, when Gerard was in England making arrangements to continue his postgraduate studies. Damian must have been visiting Cambridge for he had already finished his studies there, and Gerard often recalled Damian's courtesy and general *bonhomie* in introducing him to his first English pub at Trumpington. Later they were to meet again that same year in Kintbury where Damian was on the staff of the Juniorate.

Although they were twelve years apart in age – Gerard thirty-eight and Damian just over twenty-six – they soon found that they shared many common interests, especially their keen appreciation of English literature. Later they were to discover more common interests in drama, poetry, books in general and the particular kind of 20th century English music associated with Vaughan Williams, Delius, Butterworth and Elgar. As they were both steeped in Dickens they often continually tested one another in references and laughed about the way in which they could find themselves recalling the same favourite scenes from particular books, such as Pip and Joe Gargery comparing bites in "Great Expectations" or Sarah Gamp with her apron over her head. Indeed they even saw certain people in Dickensian terms, and this seeing characters from literature in real life situations and persons became a spin-off also of their common appreciation of Tolkien so that they shared a private understanding of certain persons as "hobbits", "elves" or "dwarves."

Their friendship developed strongly in the academic year 1970–71 when Gerard usually returned from Lancaster to the St Helens community from Friday evenings until Monday mornings. As Damian never learned to drive – he declared himself a danger to

1. Eleanor Carter, 2. Dorothy Costigan, 3. Damian Lundy at St Cassian's

Damian at Rhiw, August 1996

Louisa, Damian and Archbishop Worlock at the launch of *To Live is to Change*

Damian, Australia 1977

himself and to others even on a bicycle – Gerard was able to drive him to a number of places and events which would otherwise not have been accessible to him. They shared music and drama in Liverpool and Manchester and on a number of occasions went to Shakespeare plays at Stratford. Gerard remembers especially Damian's appreciation of the Verdi *Requiem* given in the modern, circular Liverpool Catholic cathedral with a special brass section added for the majestic *Dies Irae*. The particular acoustic of the cathedral, which resulted from its concrete and glass structure, gave unusual intensity and sonority to the brass instruments as the sound so reverberated around the imposing glass lantern that it became almost too much for some of the hearers. Not for Damian, who simply revelled in the general harmony and tumultuous sound.

Although Gerard had returned to Australia in October 1973 after serving a year in Rome as a member of the International Lasallian Centre (CIL) staff, he was a member of the International Catechetical Commission which met annually in Rome to prepare a document for the 1976 General Chapter. Members of this Commission included Brothers Herman Lombaerts, responsible at that time for the first year of the *Lumen Vitae Catechetical Institute* in Brussels, and Jeffrey Calligan, the delegate from the USA. Gerard was instrumental in introducing both of these brothers to Damian and they became close friends of his. In 1975, Damian organised what was to be the first of the Kintbury Catechetical Conferences at which Brothers Gerard and Jeffrey presented a workshop on the main lines of the document which their Commission had prepared for the forthcoming General Chapter. Damian already had a keen interest and practical experience in catechetics and in their years together at St Helens had been a most important reader and commentator on the chapters of Gerard's thesis on catechesis and religious education as it developed. Indeed, Damian's own later theological and doctoral studies grew out of these stimulating discussions of the 70's. In proposing his doctoral research at Manchester University he wrote:

With Gerard Rummery (an Australian member of our religious institute whose PhD thesis at Lancaster University was concerned with religious education in a pluralist society) I have explored a few questions related to my proposed area of research in our joint book *Growing into Faith* (Darton, Longman and Todd, London 1982), a popular work intended to help teachers and parents of teenagers.

After the opening of the Kintbury Pastoral Centre in 1975, Gerard arranged for Damian to come to Australia for nearly three months in the summer of 1977 to see the Retreat Centre at Cronulla in Sydney which had been running for some years. As Gerard himself had been invited to arrange a series of workshops in various dioceses to prepare for the 1977 Roman Synod on "Catechesis in Our Time", it was possible for Damian to work with him during the months of June, July and August. After Damian had experienced some weeks in the Cronulla Retreat Centre near Sydney, the two friends teamed up and spent the next eight to nine weeks in Australia and New Zealand working mainly with teachers and adults who were interested in the religious education of young people. They also presented a week together in the National Pastoral Centre in Melbourne.

It was particularly in these weeks on the road, meeting new groups every couple of days and travelling what to Damian were extraordinary distances by road and by air, that each came to a deeper appreciation of the other's gifts and talents. This was brought out when Damian became ill at one stage and Gerard had to take over his presentations. Later the situation was the reverse and Damian took over what Gerard usually presented. This emergency situation eventually led them to develop team teaching and present together. In a letter written to Gerry Markland from Auckland on 11th September 1977 Damian says of this first long working experience in Australia and New Zealand:

I've really enjoyed the last three months. It's been hard work at times but I've had magnificent opportunities to meet many fine people and see a great deal of Australia. Working with

Gerard Rummery has been great – we've been doing a kind of double act in many places as "the two Ronnies of Catechetics" and have based a number of the presentations and workshops on the pattern of tag wrestling: in and out of the ring every fifteen or twenty minutes! The novel method has opened up new possibilities for team teaching which I hope to follow up with Dominic and Joe at St. Cassian's.

Since Damian was very corpulent in those days, it is easy to guess which one of *The Two Ronnies* Damian played with his inimitable mixture of seriousness and comedy. But this new dynamic meant that they never presented the same material in the same way to any of the groups with whom they worked. Some very creative opening exercises were developed which were highly successful in helping the group members to be at home with one another and with the presenters. This kind of creativity sometimes had some remarkable moments which have often been recalled by those who participated in the programmes. One of them frequently cited was an audio-visual with slides and music which was devised to introduce a programme on sacraments at the National Pastoral Institute. The basic text was a letter from Dietrich Bonhoeffer's *"Letters and Papers from Prison"* in which the author addressed a letter to his nephew on the occasion of his baptism, knowing that only later would the child understand more fully what his uncle had written. Damian did the reading with that great sensitivity for words which was one of his greatest gifts while Gerard made use of one of the recurring melodies from Respighi: *"Ancient Airs and Dances"* as a kind of wistful *ostinato* which suggested both joy and sadness as part of the treadmill of life. It was only after this rich cultural experience that the deep sense of sacraments as indispensable stages of the Christian life was developed. As part of their presentations Damian and Gerard were often deepening the participants' understanding of the *"Directory for Masses with Children"* which had appeared only some years earlier. This often gave Damian scope to suggest ways of preparing liturgies and paraliturgical ceremonies with young people. It was a measure of the success of the overall programme, presented with varying emphases in some twelve to thirteen dioceses in Australia and New Zealand during this time, that Damian was so many times invited back to Australia and New Zealand for follow-up programmes in subsequent years.

Among the many memories of this time, there are some which are particularly typical of Damian's sensitivity, ready wit and repartee, indispensable qualities for any good trouper! One country diocese organised its sessions in holiday chalets beside the Pacific Ocean and, in the Australian winter north of Sydney, there were wonderfully sunny days. Another group sharing the facilities turned out to be some business men in formal suits and ties, learning transcendental meditation. This discovery excited one elderly nun, who, in full habit, confided to Damian at the breakfast table:

> "Brother Damian, do you realise that all these men in formal suits are actually doing transcendental meditation. Imagine, suits and ties at the beach in sunny weather like this! Isn't it strange?"
> "Well, Sister," said Damian, " I wonder what they are thinking about you!"
> "What do you mean?" asked Sister. "Well," answered Damian, "I wonder what they're thinking about you being here at the beach in your habit!"

On another occasion at the beginning of a workshop, it was evident that the opening night included a strong group of conservative Catholics who had come to sniff out any heresy. The workshop nature of the conference was something quite different for them, however, since so much of the early dynamic was on listening to some of the letters to the forthcoming Synod which we had been inviting young people to write wherever we worked with them. This led one of the most redoubtable and well known heresy hunters say to Damian at the end: "Brother Lundy, you're not as bad as you are made out to be", to which Damian in his most charming way replied, "Neither are you!"

The mind moves easily to another of Damian's famous repartees in England when, after addressing a group of Brothers from another religious congregation about the renewal which the Vatican Council had launched, one elderly member who had become increasingly restive as the day wore on, suddenly sprang to his feet, seething with indignation and questioned: *"Are all the De La Salle Brothers like you?"* *"No,"* said Damian, smilingly, *"we have some like you!"*

As one series of presentations involved workshops in four country dioceses in Australia, Gerard's father travelled with them for part of the way, Damian was taken to visit the Pokolbin wine growing area to offer him the chance of some wine tasting. At one of the wineries which offered lunch, the menu included a kind of traditional Australian bread, baked in the coals of a fire, called a "damper". In these days when cholesterol was not yet the watchword it has since become, Gerard's father showed Damian that the way to eat this bread, still hot from the coals, was to cut it open and allow some – no, plenty of butter – to melt inside. Between the wine tasting and the "damper", lunch became somewhat more prolonged than had been intended. Damian often recalled this journey – *"we travelled distances which for me seemed unimaginable"* – and greatly enjoyed Gerard's father pointing out aspects of the countryside through which they travelled.

Damian loved the new experiences which were part of his Australian visits. It was on one of these visits that he had his first experience of flying in a small plane from the city of Newcastle to Sydney, a distance of barely 100 miles. After finishing a two day workshop, the organisers, knowing Damian's interest in exotic meals, took him to an Indian restaurant noted for its authentic curries and from thence to the plane. In the meantime, however, what is known in Australia as a "southerly buster", a weather change from the colder south preceded by very strong winds, had arrived and the small commuter plane carrying three to four passengers, had to fly directly into it. Gerard was waiting for him at the airport in Sydney as usually the trip was only thirty minutes. Time passed, the airport personnel became distinctly uneasy until there was corroboration that the plane was landing. The four passengers staggered off the plane, one person having to be transported in a wheelchair after a flight in which the pilot was unable to climb above the wind and where the ground speed had been reduced to about half. Damian had turned a dreadful colour and after a washroom had been found he was violently sick. Gerard drove him to a nearby community which was able to provide him with a bed for the night because he felt that his stomach was still too uncertain for him to feel confident about travelling even an hour in a car. He afterwards laughed this off by saying that the Indian chef who made the "special curry" for him had told him that this would be a powerful aphrodisiac for him and the shaking up in the plane had certainly helped his resistance to temptation!

Damian, as all his friends remember, had a keen interest in different accents. He quickly noted some of the more subtle regional variations in Australian speech and really chortled over a small village he came across out in the country spelt *Clangothlin* which he quickly realised was probably named by a Welshman, homesick for *Llangollen*. He was also fascinated by the presence of so many statues of Queen Victoria (looking decidedly *"not amused"* as he loved to remark) in country parts of Australia and even more so in New Zealand. Indeed, he often remarked that Victoriana was even more widespread in Australia and New Zealand than in England.

This first Australia-New Zealand experience was an important step in Damian's life. He had to work and present himself and his ideas in different cultures to different audiences. His contribution was greatly esteemed wherever he went. He would later recognise that this first overseas mission in Australia and New Zealand of nearly three months, followed by a month in the USA as he returned to England, was a time where he collected new ideas, heard new music, saw other ways of doing things. It was a time of personal enrichment and significant growth which confirmed his basic orientations in working both with young people and with adults. His innate creativity led him to adapt many such experiences and apply them to the subsequent development of Kintbury.

During this trip to the USA, Damian was to make his first visit to the Plano Retreat Center outside Chicago. The meeting with Brother Leo Jones, an experienced member of the Plano team, was to have important repercussions for the development of the Kintbury Centre, as Leo came to work in Kintbury for some months each year. It was this contact which first led Damian to envisage the possibility of young people as members of the Kintbury team and later led to some young members of the Kintbury team having a lengthy experience as members of the Plano team.

After Gerard's posting to the International Lasallian Centre in Rome in 1978 there were many other occasions when these two friends could work closely together. This they did through many different sessions on religious education and catechesis at Kintbury as well as taking part in a number of the Loughborough Summer Schools. It was their common interest in the work of James W. Fowler which led them to sponsor Fowler's first visit to England for a national conference which took place at Newman College, Birmingham.

The Fowler visit had its amusing side. As Gerard drove Damian to Heathrow to meet Fowler, who was arriving from the USA, he asked Damian the name and number of the flight which they were to meet. It was at this stage that Gerard, a much more seasoned traveller, realised that this flight would land, not at Heathrow but at Gatwick. They quickly found a phone booth and eventually managed to get a message to the airline to assure Fowler that he was being met but that the welcoming party would be delayed. As they sped towards Gatwick as best they could in the days before there was the M25 motorway, Gerard reminded Damian that Fowler was Methodist and therefore the welcome planned at Kintbury for the next few days prior to going to Birmingham should not have any liquor. On the return journey, however, the guest speaker having been successfully met, Damian was reassured to find that the charming James Fowler was not averse to partaking of a glass of wine since the Lord himself had given us the example.

Besides sharing a number of sessions of adult education together Damian and Gerard enjoyed other experiences of music and drama. Perhaps the most vivid memory of these years was the experience of *"The Mysteries"* done by the Royal Shakespeare Company at the old Lyceum theatre in London. This combination of some of the morality plays from the Wakefield and other cycles lasted all day with *Creation & Fall* in the morning, *Preaching & Passion* in the early afternoon, and *Resurrection & Last Judgement* in the early evening. The realism of the Last Judgement scene in the final play extended to some of the promenaders being swept protesting into Hell's Mouth, Damian chortling with glee as one rather distinguished individual, carrying a *Marks and Spencer* shopping bag, was bundled down out of sight in spite of his own protests.

There was also opportunity for some summer excursions as Gerard's work in Rome often finished in May or early June. One late summer in the early 1980's, after they had been working together in the "Yes Weeks", they went by car to East Anglia together to see the famous wool churches and the scene of some of the Constable's paintings, including *Flatford Mill*. They stayed at a cottage in the Fens and from there made excursions to various places including Peterborough and Lincoln cathedrals and, of course, to Ely, which Damian had often visited from Cambridge. Damian also used the opportunity to try out a number of the "real" ales which were then coming into favour. Damian liked recalling how they distinguished themselves one Sunday morning by presenting themselves at some Anglican church whose notice board had indicated that there was a Catholic Mass. They found the congregation unusually welcoming and sang up with great gusto. At some stage, however, they realised that they were in an Anglican Series 3 celebration but decided to continue to promote ecumenism by their presence and participation. As they left the church, they explained their error to a somewhat crestfallen rector who had thought he had two recruits for the choir.

Gerard's special memory is that of a midterm break with Damian around October 1972 when they spent some days at

Rhiw in North Wales with two other members of the community. Gerard, who had just submitted his thesis, recalls being in just the right mood to appreciate the vivid autumn colours of that particular year as they drove down through the Vale of Clwyd made famous by Hopkins' nature poetry. Damian revelled in the scenery, the Welsh speaking children and their lilting English, but especially the little village of Aberdaron where the poet R.S. Thomas was then living. It was here, as they both looked over to Bardsey Island ("The island of a thousand saints") that Damian read aloud a number of Thomas's poems. For the next twenty-five years they were to send one another R.S. Thomas "discoveries" as more of Thomas's poems appeared. During this break at Rhiw they went as pilgrims, visiting a number of the pilgrimage churches along the North Wales coast which led down to Bardsey Island and, on returning to the cottage, Damian would plunge into preparing a sumptuous meal for his fellow pilgrims.

Kintbury sessions, as many of Damian's friends will recall, nearly always included, before or after the work itself, a visit by the staff or visiting lecturers to *"The Boot"*, a pub in a remote part of the "Lost Country" near the border of Berkshire, Wiltshire and Hampshire, past Combe Hill and the gallows made famous at the end of *Tess of the D'Urbervilles*. The trip was always memorable because the road was very narrow and the hedges on either side were easily some twenty feet high. If another car was encountered some backing and filling took place until a passing place could be agreed on. The pub itself was one of those very old low beamed houses which require particular caution to avoid bumping heads or tripping over unexpected stairs. It was not difficult to associate it in its remoteness with hide-and-seek games between smugglers and excise men since it was, as the crow flies, not very far from the south coast. If the remoteness made the place exotic, it was the landlord, Chris, who made it even more memorable. Chris, it seems, had been for many years associated with Salisbury Cathedral and had what seemed to be such a never ending stream of anecdotes about Salisbury diocesan affairs that it sounded like a long running Trollope serial. Damian, as all his friends remember so well, had a keen ear for accents and a great ability to mimic them so that many friends can probably recall being told about this unusual pub and its even more unusual landlord many times before they met the real character. Having heard Damian "take off" Chris the landlord so often, it was quite a shock to actually meet him and be greeted with his effusive "My dear boy!" just as Damian had imitated him.

The Chris stories are legion but it was the particular spark between Damian and Chris that made them so memorable. Chris probably believed that Damian was a clergyman of some importance, as were most of the friends whom he brought to the pub, and he eagerly cooperated with his idea that, since even the clergy needed a place for letting their hair down, he would be discreet in affording them the possibility. That was why he loved to tell stories about Archdeacon – and Canon – and their particular foibles. Damian recalled one famous Sunday summer afternoon, before the present licensing laws came into operation, when he brought some visitors at around two o'clock only to find Chris in peremptory mood, behaving as if he were a complete stranger, and pointing out that the law allowed him to serve sandwiches but no liquor. Damian, more than a little surprised, did not expostulate but sat outside with his friends to eat the sandwiches. Shortly afterwards, the only other persons present left in their car. Once they were out of sight, Chris came outside and began apologising. "My dear boy!" he said, "please forgive me, but" – indicating the direction which the car had just taken – "there were strangers present. Allow me to offer you and your friends the hospitality which you so undoubtedly deserve after your morning's labours but which these infernal laws deny you."

Damian did succeed in getting Chris and his wife to come to Kintbury for a meal one day. I think Damian himself may have done the cooking. If his idea was to give Chris a better idea of who Damian and his friends were, it seemed to have almost the opposite effect, as Damian found on a subsequent visit that there was, on Chris's part, much surreptitious winking which suggested that Damian need not worry: he was quite prepared to be discreet!

Some of Damian's friends wondered whether he had not furnished Chris with a Catholic appendage to his Salisbury anecdotes.

Gerard continued to be Damian's chauffeur on many other occasions both in England and in various places in Europe. Somehow, each occasion had something memorable about it because of Damian's deep interest in so many things. It was simply another aspect of what Brother Joseph Hendron highlighted in his tribute to Damian at his funeral in Littlemore, namely, his almost instinctive way of serving others unobtrusively simply by his presence. Damian had the gift of creating community around him by his cheerful greeting *"Cheers!"*, by his way of being present to people, of being able to listen to them and have them know that they were being listened to. Certainly, the many hours spent in the particularly captive situation of cars, enabled him to share enthusiasms with others and often to profit from another's insights.

Gerard remembers that this openness to others made working with Damian frustrating at times unless he could be freed from his many other responsibilities, especially as the Kintbury Centre developed and expanded. So many people wished to maintain contact that there were always phone calls and unexpected visitors each time these two friends had come together to do something. Gerard writes:

> It was my privilege – and, at times, my frustration – to work with Damian on the little book called *Growing into Faith*. I had written the plan and the basic text for each chapter. The "frustration" came about because Damian was so generous with his time for others that it became very difficult for him to find the time to sit down and give himself a few days, let alone a few weeks, of concentrated work. He never really did learn to say "No!" when he was phoned to take on new work. But I can remember his reading of my original draft and then, with great tact, suggesting that perhaps we could add something " like this". I would scribble furiously as he spoke, very much aware that what I was hearing was vintage Damian, and it was important not to lose one of his ideas. In those pre-computer days, this usually meant my typing up a new version and then

trying to corner him again long enough to see what he thought. When I look at the text now I can recognise his insights instantly and can admire his ability to make profound truths sound simple.

Growing into Faith grew out of our shared conviction that, as Damian would often, say, "What young people are rejecting often is Churchianity rather than Christianity!" Through his deep love and knowledge of Scripture, he often tried to help others to read the Gospel anew and see the person of Jesus through new eyes. That is why it was his closely annotated and increasingly battered Jerusalem Bible, with all kinds of separate sheets sticking out of it, which was the first thing that went with him when he travelled.

It was Damian's involvement in so many other things that eventually prevented the completion of the sequel to *Growing into Faith,* as Gerard recalls:

I remember a lunch with the late John Todd of Darton, Longman and Todd, who pleaded with us to write the second book which we had already envisaged as a follow-up to *Growing into Faith.* Although we had not decided on a title as such, it was to be about Religion and Faith as these two "cousins" are experienced in the lives of young people in a modern society. We did write the ground plan together and I had written two chapters prior to 1986 when I was elected to the General Council of my congregation. Our plan was that Damian would write the more anecdotal aspects from the lives of the young persons whom he met. Some of this writing eventually ended up in the little book *What's the Point of it All?*, especially the chapters called *Sharing the Darkness*, from which I was privileged to read one of his poems at his funeral, and *A Man Born Blind*. But, in spite of all the efforts we made to finish the book, Damian could never resist responding to the many people who called on him, and my own duties in Rome never again furnished the opportunity for us to complete the work as we had done with *Growing into Faith*. In a personal inscription when he sent me a copy of *What's the Point of it All?*, Damian wrote: "Gerard, this book contains a couple of the pieces which were to have been included in the second book we nearly wrote together! "

There was a certain sense that, as Damian's world expanded, he found it increasingly difficult to refuse anyone who asked for his help. Other close friends who worked with Damian in the *National Project*, the Vatican II booklet *To live is to Change* and other projects, will easily sympathise with the following tribute:

> His presence affected many people and his light burned brightly – perhaps too brightly for his body to cope with. I never remember him doing one thing, talking about one project or planning just one seminar or book – everything was in multiples. And yet through it all he had time for me – at that time just a foot soldier, always there as I rose through the ranks with kind words of encouragement in dark moments.

If this was, in a certain sense at least, the downside of Damian becoming an international person, developing friendship with so many people and consequently having far too many calls made on him, it was also the Damian who never hesitated to share with others the richness of his own experience.

6 | Damian: Poet, Hymn Writer and Liturgist

Damian is probably known by many people as a hymn writer but, if his hymns are worth remembering, it was first of all because the content of so many of his hymns is memorable: he was a very good poet. Mind you, as one of his close friends reminds us, Damian rarely used the word *hymns:* he preferred *songs.* Notice that the subtitle of his *Songs of the Spirit* was *Songs and Hymns of Renewal.* It was almost as though he feared that hymns would be limited to churches, whereas he saw his songs as contributing to living life fully and not simply in church. He never saw himself as talented musically and was known to describe himself in a classic put-down, as being like Bottom in *A Midsummer Night's Dream,* having " *a good ear for the tongs and the bones."* Certainly he had little training in music, could not play any instrument but did have a good sense of rhythm, was reliable in pitch and easily made up by enthusiasm what he may have lacked in finesse. Brother Thomas Campbell, former provincial who lived eight years with Damian in the same community, remarks on this:

> I found it extraordinary that someone so naturally musical – he certainly knew a good tune as well as he knew a bad one – had gone through life without any musical training, even the most basic. I never once saw him sit at a piano, let alone hammer out a tune.

But what musical talent he had was exploited to the full. Many of his first hymns were originally composed for the community celebrations in the Juniorate where the main participants, apart from the staff, were croaky voiced adolescents whose singing gamut was not much more than within the octave from middle C. With the coming of the guitar as the usual form of accompaniment, it was both easier to adjust pitch to adolescent voices as well as to provide a basic underlying rhythm which kept the melody moving at a good pace. Thus it was that in a forty-five minute practice time once per week with the Junior novices, Damian launched his musical career.

Sometimes the hymns were adaptations of good melodies (Damian would certainly have agreed with Luther's question: *"Why should the devil have all the best tunes?"*). The original tune which he offered to the Juniors for his very fine text of *The wind was cold one April morning*, was that of *Shenandoah!* Of course, the melody in the published edition of the first collection of *Songs of the Spirit* was composed by Hubert Richards. It is worth recalling that this was the era of the liturgy in English, the coming of the guitar in churches, and the publication of much material in a folk song or ballad style – St. Louis Jesuits, Weston Priory, the Beatles, Pete Seeger, Joan Baez etc. Damian, fresh from his years in Cambridge, was full of energy and ready to share with everyone. These years in the Juniorate gave him both a place and a community where the very liturgical year he was living with these Junior novices continually presented the challenge of celebrating the new vernacular liturgy with them. Moreover, he had much more freedom with the resident chaplain (Father O'Keefe) than was possible in many parishes at the same time. Besides making use of many fine hymns once thought of as "non-Catholic" (*Bread of Heaven, When I survey the wondrous Cross* etc.) Damian felt the need to offer these young fourteen to sixteen year olds something which was closer to them and to their immediate understanding than were many of the traditional hymns sung in Catholic parishes at the time, such as Father Faber's *"Daily, daily sing to Mary"* and *"Sweet Sacrament Divine"*.

Damian's hymns were based on Scripture. In the preface which he wrote to the first volume of *Songs of the Spirit* he expressed his idea of what a good hymns should be.

"I believe a good hymn should offer thoughts and images to nourish personal prayer and reflection, as well as being a vehicle of communal praise. The best words and images are scriptural. The music sets the mood of a hymn and so helps to determine the atmosphere of the celebration."

In his introduction to *Songs of the Spirit 3*, he reminds his readers "that Vatican II's Constitution on the Sacred Liturgy declares:

Composers, filled with the Holy Spirit, should feel that their vocation is to cultivate sacred music and increase its store of treasures and that the texts intended to be sung must always be in conformity with Catholic doctrine: indeed they should be drawn chiefly from Holy Scripture and from liturgical sources.

In commending the later composite edition entitled *Best of Songs of the Spirit*, Damian's Foreword concludes by saying:

Since almost all the lyrics are Scriptural in their words and images, my prayer is that they may continue to nourish the personal faith, hope and love of individual Christians and of communities who use the new collection.

A complete list of Damian's hymns in the three volumes of *Songs of the Spirit* (referred to henceforth as SS1, SS2 and SS3) shows that the Scriptural hymns are far more numerous than the others although it is worth noting at least three separate categories among these hymns. First of all, there were the hymns where the scriptural text itself provides him with the content and he was content to adapt it only inasmuch as was necessary to fit the basic structure of the musical form. Two fine examples of this are SS1, 75, based on Ephesians 3, *This then is my prayer* and Damian's wonderful text in SS2, 168, which begins *If I am lacking love*, based on 1 Corinthians, 13. In others, sometimes but not always, following a borrowing from the original French, he merges verses from similar but separate psalms to give a particular emphasis. Some very good examples of this from SS1 are *Lord, however can I repay you* (6) and *All glory to you* (31), both adapted from the French original text and music of R. Jef, and *In your coming and your going* (46) with D. Julien's original music. A third category are those many hymns where the scriptural incident provides him with the basic story to which he adds his own *"composition of place"* in the best Ignatian manner. It is significant that although some of Damian's compositions are typically four-square chorale style hymns, the ones for which he is best remembered tend to be looser in form and are more likely to depend on elements such as syncopation and natural speech rhythms rather than on metric perfection.

Damian's many settings of the psalms, including his adaptations from French composers, are also remarkable for his sureness as regards English speech rhythms and the need to have the necessary complementarity between words and music. One such gem is *"Lord, however can I repay you?"*, a text based on Psalms 114 and 115, to a melody by the French composer Raymond Jef. Another is the fine Easter hymn which begins *"You who sleep rise up"* even though Damian himself later felt that the opening words *"You who..."* were unfortunate as they sometimes provoked mirth among the singers.

Damian was not simply an adapter: very often his work improved the original. One good example from many others of such improvement of a fine hymn by the addition of more scriptural passages is the text of the three verses which he added to Jimmy Owens' hymn *In love for me* (SS2, 195). Damian's words build on the two earlier Eucharistic verses. *Back to my Father, soon I shall go* recalls growth in the Spirit through John's gospel image of the vine and branches, and he concludes with *Love one another* through *serving one another*. The whole hymn then speaks not only of the institution of the Eucharist but also of the practical way in which all are challenged by this great love of Christ to love others more deeply by serving Christ in them.

In his Eulogy at Damian's funeral Mass at Littlemore, Brother Joseph Hendron drew attention to Damian's deep appreciation of Liturgy and everything associated with it:

> The documents of Vatican II were coming on stream. Those on liturgical renewal were of particular interest to Damian, since he saw Liturgy as a key element in all worthwhile renewal. Without delay he set about implementing them. This was no mere rearranging of furniture; primarily it was aimed at people – at helping people live the new insights.

Damian's vision, based on his keen appreciation of the Vatican II document on Revelation, *Dei Verbum*, was the importance of the "now", the "here and now" of the saving God who continues to reveal himself through word and event. Hence, the ritual had to be made relevant to this moment, to this celebration, to this congregation, so that due importance was given to the use of sign and symbol and posture and gesture. Since, in his judgement, the senses had to be stimulated, sight, sound, touch and gesture were indispensable concomitants of this process as well as candles, lights, banners, incense. There was an important sense in which he saw every prayer, every celebration, not simply as the carrying out of a duty or a ritual but as something which was always a unique moment, an unrepeatable moment in the lives of all the participants.

This keen sense of God's *saving plan* is the keynote of most of his hymns in that they usually have an historical perspective. They frequently sing of some incident from the history of salvation, as for example in O *Mary when our God chose you* (SS1, 53) where the first three verses depict scenes from the stable at Bethlehem, but then move naturally from there to our present *barren world, to its empty streets and broken hearts* to pray that *all his brothers* will follow Jesus home. Many other examples from SS1 come readily to mind, such as the verses Damian wrote to *Walk in the Light* (15), *Mother of God's Living Word* (41), *How good it is to know your Name* (43) and *Lord Jesus Christ* (88). Sometimes the scriptural and salvation history motifs are both present, as in *Sing the Good News* (SS2, 155), inspired by *Romans 10:14* and by the outline of a new religious education programme entitled *Becoming Good News* worked on by Brother Jeffrey Calligan and some Brothers from the USA.

As has already been mentioned, this felicitous blending of words and already existing music was typical of many of Damian's hymns. His many hymns in honour of the Blessed Virgin are new texts fitted to a suitable melody. But there is always a "present tense" about them which Damian wished to share with others, probably in response to the reaction of the Junior novices to some of the more sentimental traditional Marian hymns. This attention to the here and now of God's great saving plan remains part of their attractiveness. Some of these melodies come from other countries, especially France, in which Damian passed a formative period as a young Brother. Others are based on traditional English tunes. A particularly fine example is SS1, 13, *"Sing of a Girl"* for the feasts of Mary's birthday. It recalls the tradition that she was presented in the Temple. The tune is based on the folk song *"Strawberry Fair."* Each of the seven verses evokes in a few words the chosen Mary of the Temple, the mother Mary in the stable at Bethlehem, the *Pietà*, a meeting after the Resurrection, the Mary in the Cenacle at Pentecost and the enduring Madonna of Christian devotion. While the song undoubtedly takes some of its appeal from the simple melody, it is the fine blending of Scriptural and traditional images in such an economy of words which impresses those who meet it for the first time and those who continue to sing it. It is strong piety, not sentimentality, which keeps reminding us of *the child that mother will bear.*

Another outstanding Mary song (SS2, 102) for which Damian wrote both words and music, *When Mary listened to God's word,* is a brilliant evocation of the Annunciation by the Angel Gabriel. If both text and music impress by their simplicity, it is because of the few strokes needed by the author to place us immediately within the scene with Mary, to hear again scriptural words familiar to us from the narratives of the Annunciation and Mary's canticle at the Visitation. The simple petition which concludes the hymn comes almost as an instinctive response to this contemplation.

We are privileged to have from Damian's collected papers another *Annunciation* poem which was never set to music:

That quiet girl whose eyes are lowered
Listens intently for a sign.
The only sign's the listening,
The half closed eyes..." Whose baby? Mine?"

"No, his!" No – his! The Holy one
Whose word has found an ear in you!
So listen – and let his power be
The life within your body now.

Yield to his love! That power must be
An awesome, penetrating rain.
And in her heart the quiet girl knows
Our Lord, and trembles at the pain;

And in her eye a tear is formed.
Her lips to shape an answer part:
"Your child and mine? Then let it be."
A shadow falls across her heart.

Quietly the messenger retires,
Letting the comfort soothe the fear;
Bows to his Lord within the girl,
Starts at the smile beneath the tear.

This is a remarkable poem in its theological depth, its conciseness and in its ability to show the humanity of the Mary who said "Yes." It has its own overtones, redolent of many memorable metaphysical poems such as George Herbert's *Love bade me welcome*. The text cries out for the beauty and subtlety of a Vaughan Williams musical setting such as this most English of musicians achieved with his *Five Mystical Songs*.

Those who were able to assist at the Commemoration Mass of July 2nd in London will recall that Damian's previously unpublished hymn on *The Visitation* was given its first public performance on that day. The text of this poem is included in the Appendix.

Special mention should be made of the fine texts of hymns which celebrate various aspects of the great mysteries celebrated in Holy Week. Many of these hymns were written or adapted to help the young men at Kintbury share more deeply in the great events of the celebration of the Passion and Resurrection. It may well be that Damian's approach in his original version of *"The wind was cold"* (SS1,3) was consciously or unconsciously influenced at that time by Sidney Carter's fine marriage of words and music in his Passion hymn *"I danced in the morning"*, or Damian's own love for the Glasgow Orpheus Choir's singing of *"All in the April evening."* In any case, the folk song style with its overall repeating pattern of *"and while he said goodbye, blew the wind in April"* contains some of Damian's most vividly terse poetical images. The original version, consisting of the first four verses with its poignant *"They laid him in the garden,"* was later extended by two more verses to include a beautiful evocation of the Resurrection. A similar intensity is found in *"One cold night in spring"* (SS1,84), in *"The night before our Saviour died"* (SS1, 24) and in the traditional *"Reproaches"* (SS1,56) which he adapted for Good Friday. Besides helping others to appreciate the profound mysteries commemorated in these hymns, Damian reveals a great deal of his own deep faith, reverence and devotion through the appropriateness and sheer clarity of these hymns. His keen eye for a telling phrase which communicates something of the mystery that is the truth of Easter is shown in his translation of the French text of *"New daytime dawning"* (SS1,62) with its imagery of spring and the risen Christ *"with arms wide"* standing *"in the garden"* where *"the door is open wide"* and where now *"there's no need to hide."* Indeed, this contrast between the garden of the Fall and the place where Christ's Resurrection is made known comes through in a number of his songs. Yes, there is something pedagogical about them as well, since he was often trying to help adolescent boys enter into these profound mysteries since it was so typical of Damian to wish to share with others what he himself had contemplated.

Religious communities, schools and Kintbury groups will undoubtedly have their own preferences when it is a question of Damian's scriptural hymns. Few, however, will dispute the enduring importance and popularity of his *Song for a Young Prophet* (SS1, 20), the evocation of the vocation of the prophet in the first chapter of Jeremiah. As regards content, there is the brilliance of the poetic text which even in its paraphrasing never loses the intensity of the original. Then there is the wonderful complementarity of words and melody where natural speech stresses and music continually illuminate one another. How interesting, therefore, to hear the genesis of this hymn as it is recalled by Brother Nicholas Hutchinson speaking of the involvement of Lasallian Resource in various Charismatic Conferences:

> It was at one of those Conferences that 'O, *the word of my Lord*' was written... Damian had asked for accommodation such that the group could interact more readily. Gathered one evening, Damian and several others (particularly Gerry Markland) sat and played various combinations of notes until the final version was agreed upon of what became the very popular hymn, 'tried out' the next day by all the participants of the Conference.

It was this *Song for a Young Prophet* which was sung so movingly at the Ninian Park meeting with Pope John Paul.

This last anecdote reminds us that one of the enduring aspects of Damian's own work as hymn writer and adapter was the inspiration and encouragement which he provided for others. This was particularly so in the preparation of the three volumes of *Songs of the Spirit*, nearly 300 hymns in all. As his own preface to the first collection of *Songs of the Spirit* so clearly shows, he certainly had his own idea as to what a good hymn was but he was in no way opposed to what others had done. While this meant profiting from the many popular collection of hymns of the 1960's and 1970's such as the St Louis Jesuits, Celebration Services, Carey Landry and the North American Liturgy Resources, he also encouraged various people, especially musicians who came to Kintbury, to write or arrange music for him. As Lasallian Resource was formed, he recognised talent in the young musicians whom he came to know and gladly accepted their own work. Important contributions were made by Christine McCann, Gerard Markland, Maria Parkinson, Anne-Marie Walsh and Anthony Sharpe and others whose names can be seen throughout the three volumes of *Songs of the Spirit*. Damian recognised this indispensable contribution when he wrote in his preface to the first collection:

> Most of all I am indebted to my friends who sing these hymns at various liturgical gatherings and renewal conferences, especially those organised at Hopwood Hall. Our group was once named 'RentaMass' but we prefer to call ourselves 'Lasallian Resource', for everyone either belongs to the De La Salle Brothers or is a close friend and associate of our Lasallian family... Songs of the Spirit would never have been published without more than a little help from my friends. With love I dedicate it to them.

Gerard Markland remembers that

> we worked on about half a dozen hymns together. I'd usually think up a tune with a few lines of scripture to go with it and then send it off to Damian who would write out the verses. But two hymns stand out, *Do not be afraid* and *I will be with you*. I've always thought that Damian's influence in these two hymns was far more than just being the one who was very gifted with words and scripture. It was much deeper and personal... I'd written *Do not be afraid* – the tune and the first couple of verses – but it remained unsung, on a scrap of paper... During the conference later that year at Kintbury, Damian split us into groups to prepare for the liturgy for the day. So I trotted off, guitar in hand, to join Damian and the music group. After mulling over various hymn books for about 20 minutes, I very sheepishly mentioned that I had written something that we might be able to use. After immediate encouragement from Damian, I proceeded to play the chorus and the first couple of verses of *Do not be afraid*. Straight away Damian said, 'That is going to be a national hit!' Thinking that this was just Damian at his

exuberant best, we all got carried away with his excitement and proceeded to add a couple more verses to the hymn. And so, late that day in the 'Upper Room' at St Cassian's not only was *Do not be afraid* born but also my gift of song writing... I wrote *I will be with you* a year later in 1977. By this time I had decided to leave the Brothers and as a result of this Damian wrote a wonderful letter to me. It expressed all that I loved about Damian – his humour, sympathy and understanding, hope and encouragement, his literary gifts and his love and concern. For all those feelings and emotions to sweep over me at a time when I was feeling very unsure about the next step was a very poignant moment for me. Suffice to say that I picked up my guitar straight away and began to write the music for *I will be with you.*

His visits to Australia and New Zealand and his continuing contacts with Rome as a member of the International Catechetical Commission 1978–1981, as a participant in the International Lasallian Centre in 1979 and as a member of the Rule Commission in 1984, broadened his experience of music from the Italian and Spanish cultures. *Laudato Sii* and *Look at the Sky* were translated and rearranged after he fell in love with Assisi during his first visit in 1979. Australian Frank Anderson's *Father in my life I see* with its canon form, one of the great successes led by Lasallian Resources at Ninian Park for the Papal Visit of 1983, was first heard by Damian during a visit to Australia in 1981 and included in the second book of *Songs of the Spirit*. *Songs of the Spirit 3* included another five of Frank Anderson's scriptural songs.

It is not possible to separate Damian's hymn writing and selection from his role of leadership in liturgy. He had a keen eye for a telling citation, a paragraph, a good text which brought new insights into a well known truth. When he himself read, he had a particular ability to "point" the text in a way which often arrested the attention and brought deeper meaning to his hearers. He was insistent that readers should prepare their reading carefully. This was in no way simply for better elocution: he had a deep reverence for the role of breaking open the Scriptures for the community.

Another aspect of his guidance in liturgy was his ability to set the celebration in a context which respected both the sacredness of the rite to be followed and the uniqueness of this particular community gathered in faith. This gift he exercised not only by his introduction at the beginning of the ceremony but also by his ability to animate the congregation through different forms of participation – posture, gesture, singing and, in his more exuberant moments, hand clapping and movement. This was not always easily accepted by adults, although young people usually had little difficulty. In the District annual retreats made at Hopwood Hall by the Brothers of the then separate English and London Districts or Provinces, where the spacious modern chapel lent itself more easily to spontaneous movement, it took some years before all the Brother participants found themselves at ease with such innovations. It was the same with the various Charismatic Conferences and Retreats conducted at Ampleforth, Southampton and especially Hopwood Hall where Damian and Lasallian Resource gradually became, at the request of the participants themselves, an essential element of the retreat. This was acknowledged by Bishop Langton D. Fox in his Foreword to the first volume of *Songs of the Spirit:*

> "At Conferences, like the Priests' at Hopwood ('78), where they (Brother Damian Lundy and his Group, Lasallian Resource) have been in charge of the music, we have been helped by what I thought to be a healthy, Catholic balance of folk, traditional and plainsong music."

Damian and charismatic renewal

This is a suitable moment to say something more about the overall impact of the charismatic movement – the Renewal, as it was called at the time – on Damian himself, on his music and on the selections of music he made. His collections are *Songs of Renewal.* The emphases of this international movement, especially its scriptural bases and its liturgical creativity to name only two aspects, were both a source of encouragement and an important resource for the busy Damian as he worked with Joseph Hendron and Dominic Green after September 1975 in the development of the Kintbury Pastoral Centre. His participation in a number of national and (later in Rome in 1979) international meetings enlarged his own already extensive repertoire of songs and confirmed his conviction that there was a need for more spontaneous celebrations of faith. Indeed, Kintbury for many will always be associated with Damian's simple but doctrinally rich text "Walk in the light" and his unforgettable use of "Bind us together" for the final liturgy of so many Kintbury sessions. An enduring memory for many persons is also the exuberance of the dancing and cavorting Damian, plump but astonishingly agile, as his own enthusiasm led groups to more spontaneous expressions of joy and delight as they celebrated together. In August 1999 a Lasallian gathering of young people from Europe, Canada and the United States took place in Worth. Language groups took it in turn to prepare prayer and liturgy. On several occasions, without any previous consultation, the whole assembly of some 250 young people would break out spontaneously into *Walk in the Light* and sing it with great smiles on their faces, arms in the air, praising God. It was a tiny hint of Damian's impact worldwide. It was sometimes hard to get them to stop and encourage them to go and eat!

His profound conviction that God's Spirit speaks to all who gather in Jesus' name led to the creation of the Kintbury prayer room, the Quiet Room, which has continued to be for the past twenty-five years one of the indispensable elements of the Kintbury experience. It would be difficult to do justice to the importance of so many sessions of shared prayer as the participants continue to pass around the lighted candle and offer their own prayers, or to the profound silence of groups gathered together with a vivid sense of God's indwelling and presence. In all of this, however, Damian was deeply conscious of the importance of not allowing Kintbury to be simply an emotional experience, with nothing solid to it. The preparation for the post-Kintbury experience of home, school and church was a most important "decompression" exercise for him so that the young people returned home strengthened in their faith but with a clear view of the reality which they faced.

In this regard, Damian eventually maintained his own distance from the more highly emotional aspects of some charismatic sessions. After an initial experience of "being slain in the Spirit," he stood back from the more effusive manifestations of which he was wary, although always respectful. Although invited officially and with some insistence to become a member of an international group promoting the Renewal, Damian firmly declined. While he never lost his conviction about the profound importance of devotion to the Holy Spirit and retained close links with friends whom he had made through the Renewal, he imposed his own personal limits on those more extravagant aspects where he had felt that he was no longer in control.

The Papal visit to Ninian Park

The final words of Damian's Introduction to the first volume of *Songs of the Spirit* allude to the formation of Lasallian Resource. From 1973 onwards several De La Salle Brothers studying in Hopwood Hall, the College of Education under the direction of the Brothers, all offered their services in parishes in the Salford Diocese to help animate the music of the liturgy. The group expanded with friends, and a tongue-in-cheek name was coined – "Rent-a-Mass" – before becoming known as "Lasallian Resource". Of its nature the group was flexible in membership and variously included: Mary Barrett, Laurence Brigden, Mark Condron, Paul Davey, Nick Hutchinson, Damian Lundy, Gerry Markland,Christine McCann, Peter Mellor, Maria Parkinson, Anthony Sharpe and Stephen Till.

Charismatic Renewal was developing in the Catholic Church, and Lasallian Resource became the liturgical group for Hopwood Charismatic Days of Renewal, and for many Charismatic Conferences from Southampton and Ampleforth to several held at Hopwood Hall, including the Priests' Conference of 1978. Damian often gave presentations (talks) at these Conferences, as well as being one of the leaders of the music – the group worked together very well, and various roles were swapped around. Occasionally at those Conferences new hymns would be written, and other hymns would be 'tried out' further, with the intention of including at least some of them in future volumes of *Songs of the Spirit*. It was at one of the first Conferences that '*Oh the word of my Lord*' was written.

For the compilation of the first book of *Songs of the Spirit*, Damian tapped various friends for hymns. Christine McCann (author of some six to seven hymns in the different volumes of *Songs of the Spirit*) recalls how she came to be involved:

> I really got to know Damian, who had taught my younger brother, during the Caring Church Week at Notre Dame, Eccleston, St Helens. I sang the then unpublished hymn 'Gifts of Bread and Wine' and Damian heard it. He asked me to 'write the dots down' and let him have a copy. The next I knew, it was published! Without Damian none of my work would ever have got near a publisher. I will always be indebted to him for that.

Brother Nicholas Hutchinson remembers using one finger to tap out on the organ in the empty chapel of Hopwood the hymn that Maria Parkinson was singing, and he then wrote out on manuscript the melody line of her hymn, *As I kneel before you* (SS1, 7). Damian later handed him several records and tapes that he had and asked him to go through them all and select the best hymns – and so appeared Carey Landry's *Lay your hands* and *I will never forget you*, both of which found their way into *Songs of the Spirit 1*.

Lasallian resource and Ninian Park

We are also indebted to Brother Nicholas Hutchinson for the details of the following account of the role played by Lasallian Resource as one of the music groups chosen to participate in the assembly at Ninian Park, Cardiff, on the occasion of Pope John Paul's visit to Britain. This account is based on something which he wrote for the *District Newsletter* of the time, and he refreshed his memory by viewing again a video recording of the event. Some other members of Lasallian Resource who were present substantiate what follows.

Invitation to Ninian Park

A highlight of the music ministry of Lasallian Resource came with the invitation to "play for the Pope" at the gathering of Young People in Ninian Park, Cardiff, on 2 June 1982. It was the time of the Falklands War, and it remained unclear as to whether the Pope would visit Great Britain at a time of war with Argentina. Much behind-the-scenes diplomacy and activity took place to enable the visit to go ahead. The uncertainty was such that during the course of the BBC transmission from Ninian Park in the afternoon, a commentator remarked: *"It's almost impossible to believe that one short week ago we were wondering if this visit would take place."* Progress was made, it seems, by the Pope agreeing that he would visit Argentina at a later date.

Fr Ernie Sands, one of the main liturgical organisers of the Day at Ninian Park, and a good friend of Damian's, (his very popular "Come, Holy Spirit" is No. 63 in *Songs of the Spirit 1*), arranged for Lasallian Resource to lead the liturgy.

Rehearsing in Kintbury

At Damian's invitation the group stayed a couple of days in Kintbury to rehearse the music. At that time the group did not know *'We're the Church of today, the hope of tomorrow"* – the key song of the Ninian Park event, written by Fr Ernie Sands, who would be conducting from the centre spot of the ground of Ninian Park, where some 37,000 young people gathered from the dioceses of England and Wales.

On the morning of Tuesday 1st June the group travelled from Kintbury for a pre-arranged rehearsal in the stadium with the BBC sound recordists. Seeing that the number of microphones and direct leads asked of the BBC were not available for use, someone had to go and hire an independent sound system there and then. Sound testing was to have been at 1pm but it could not take place until 7pm – one of several frustrating things to occur that day. The group was provided with hotel accommodation in Cardiff on that Tuesday night by the organising committee, known as Papal Tours Limited.

The morning

Brother Nicholas remembers in vivid detail some further problems of this day:

> While the Pope was celebrating Mass in the morning at Pontcanna Fields in Cardiff, we all had Mass in Ninian Park with Cardinal Hume and the bishops of England, amidst a thunderstorm and a torrential downpour. Appropriate songs might have been 'O Living Water' and 'Let it flow through me', but there was audible laughter from the crowd as we sang 'Our God reigns'! Our contribution to the Mass included Cat Stevens' arrangement of 'Morning has broken' using the electric piano recently paid for by Brother Leander (the then Visitor, who, with Brother Victor, the previous Visitor, was always very supportive of the ministry of Lasallian Resource). We also led the 'Peruvian Gloria', 'I will be with you', 'Alleluia, sing to Jesus,' 'I am the bread of life' and 'All over the world.'
>
> I don't recall whether or not it was Damian who spoke over the public address system, introducing hymns to be practised etc, but I do remember the announcement that a senior police inspector who was responsible for security in the ground had expressed his appreciation and admiration of all the young people present, saying that he and his colleagues generally only experienced what was negative with young people. Here, without exception, they were being treated with courtesy etc, he had remarked. The young people then cheered!
>
> We had agreed amongst ourselves previously that whenever the crowd started a spontaneous rendition of "He's got the whole world in his hands', we would interrupt by starting another hymn, and this can be seen at one point in the broadcast. We felt that the words of the song would not be thought appropriate by people watching on TV, for the crowd were focussing the song on the Pope, rather than on God himself!

Brother Nicholas continues:

The Ninian Park booklet (serving both the morning Mass and the afternoon papal para-liturgy) was designed and printed as an A4 booklet folded lengthwise. It was an attractive format and was designed in that elongated form (I remember Damian saying), so that it could be held aloft and waved – as indeed it was. Union flags and Papal flags, as well as banners and scarves of orange white and blue, were also in evidence amongst the young people.

The time of the Pope's journey to Ninian Park

The weather cleared as the Pope had a midday meal at Cardiff Castle before being transported by Popemobile to Ninian Park Stadium. The BBC commentator remarked that the young people formed the largest crowd seen in this football stadium this season – poor old Cardiff City having just gone down to the Third Division.

As the Pope was travelling to the stadium, Damian's voice could be heard over the PA system, asking the young people to be aware of avoiding interrupting the Pope, especially during his sermon. Again whilst the Pope was on his journey, Lasallian Resource led the singing of "Bind us together", and Damian's voice can be heard clearly shouting out (in his characteristic way!) each line of the verses so that the crowd could join in.

The group led the singing of "I will sing, I will sing a song unto the Lord", followed by a Carribean band with their appealing metal drums. By this time, Damian had walked to the outside of the stadium, there to join about a dozen people who were lined up to greet the Pope. It was whilst Damian was standing there (the video recording reminds me) that the hymn "Father, in my life I see" was sung – the first line by girls throughout the stadium and echoed by boys; Damian heard it clearly from outside the stadium itself, and the TV broadcast presents the male/female singing quite effectively.

Just outside the stadium, the Pope was greeted first by Cardinal Hume, then a bishop and a representative six young stewards. The broadcaster mentions another person in the line – the RC Chairman of Cardiff City Football Club, who had donated the use of his stadium. (Damian mentioned that he had been told that the more impressive Arms Park (rugby) Stadium would have cost too much, and would have been of such a size that the organisers were unsure as to whether or not they would be able to fill it with young people, and they preferred to be sure of having a full stadium).

Some orchestral pieces (numbers from the musical *'Oliver'* etc.) were being played during this transition period, and the crowd sang spontaneously 'You'll never walk alone" – undoubtedly started by the contingent from the Liverpool Archdiocese.

Arrival in the stadium itself and introduction

As the Pope appeared on the specially built platform in the stadium itself, several minutes' acclamation led into another spontaneous "You'll never walk alone". As planned, Lasallian Resource started to play "Our God reigns", which the BBC commentator added was "the Pope's favourite hymn", and the video recording of the event shows clearly that the Pope persisted in looking at the group as the song started. In the introduction to the hymn, Peter Mellor's mandolin (a characteristic sound of the group) was heard very clearly, complimenting the main line of the music. John Paul sang from the text before him.

The Pope led with the Sign of the Cross and a liturgical greeting. After further applause Cardinal Hume gave a very brief welcome in which he said that he trusted "that this enthusiasm can be channelled to the service and love of God and of our country" – words that perhaps conveyed much to some people listening via TV, allaying fears and apprehensions from the four hundred year old religious feud. Perhaps some would understand that "Love of… our country" is as implicit in Catholics as in others. The 1999 obituaries of Cardinal Hume would comment that the event of the Papal Visit (as well as his own personality) helped to convey that the Roman Catholic Church in Great Britain had come out of the ghetto and had "come of age".

The song for a young prophet
(*Oh the word of my lord*) and a prayer

A teenager gave a formal address before the Pope, and a group performed liturgical dance around the 'Call of Samuel'. What followed can only be called a very beautiful rendition of "Oh the word of my Lord". It could not have been played or sung better as the group led the whole stadium in a very prayerful singing of the hymn. The video recording shows that it was sung very reverently by the people in the stadium. So striking was the transmission from Lasallian Resource over the PA system, that the BBC later took this recording and incorporated it on a BBC cassette that went on sale: effectively "the best" of Ninian Park.

To conclude this account of the celebration, undoubtedly the highlight (at least in the sense of publicity) of Damian's ministry through song, we have the following recollection of Christine McCann:

When the Pope came to Cardiff, Damian had the control of the crowds and crowds of young people totally at his fingertips by sheer dint of his charisma.

The recordings

Damian and the members of Lasallian resource had often thought about recording the three volumes of *Songs of the Spirit* as demonstration tapes. The project eventually took place in a long and memorable weekend at Kintbury. Many readers of this biography will probably treasure these cassettes not only for the quality of the music but also because they preserve the sound of Damian's voice as he introduces each song.

Recording sessions are notoriously difficult and this famous weekend at Kintbury has its own memories for those who participated. Among such memories is the following one from Christine McCann:

During all of the recordings with Lasallian Resource, I remember a laughing, rotund Brother who, if in habit, would kick his leg in the air and swish the habit around. Whatever his own state of mind, he would cheer everyone with his antics and his jokes about himself.

I recall once when recording the "I will be with you" record, we had to stand absolutely still as the last notes were sung/ played and then wait for Kevin Mayhew to turn off the machine. Somehow Damian's last note always left him either with a hand or a leg in the air or standing in some way in a precarious position... this time he overbalanced, knocked a table and all its contents flying and caused us all to shriek with laughter... and the recording had to be done all over again!

It would be difficult to estimate the contribution made by Damian and Lasallian Resource through the recording of the three volumes of *Songs of the Spirit*. Certainly, even though Lasallian Resource no longer exists, many of the songs are still sung and appreciated in many places in the British Isles and occasionally heard in BBC broadcasts or in *Songs of Praise*. But they are heard as well in Australia and New Zealand, India, Sri Lanka, Pakistan and in a number of English speaking countries in Africa. That in itself is a tribute to the quality of the songs and of course to Damian.

Damian as poet

Apart from the texts of the hymns which he composed, Damian was also a considerable poet in his own right. Some of his finest poetry is to be found in these hymns, in the freshness of a new translation or in the graphic down-to-earth development of a profound theological truth. This attention to content sometimes led him to be very impatient when someone arbitrarily selected only certain verses of a hymn in a way which disregarded its inner structure and coherence.

Tributes from Damian's literature students, wherever he taught, are unanimous in their admiration for his profound insights, especially in poetry. As already mentioned, he had the ability to help others **listen** to poetry with the ear and not simply scan it with the eye. He illuminated many of his workshops by a line or phrase which conveyed a profound truth. R. S.Thomas's *The Moon in Lleyn* is a good example:

In cities that
have outgrown their promise people
are becoming pilgrims
again, if not to this place,
then to the recreation of it
in their own spirits.

One of his favourite poems when he was dealing with parents or teachers who were having difficulty with young people was C. Day Lewis's *Walking away* with its image of Lewis's son walking away from his father on his first day at boarding school, especially the concluding lines:

I have had worse partings, but none that so
Gnaws at my mind still. Perhaps it is roughly
saying what God alone can perfectly show.
How selfhood begins with a walking away
and love is proved in the letting go.

When he was asked to be godfather to Alastair, the son of Shona and David Tildesley, Damian not only graced Alistair's baptism by his presence, but wrote the following beautiful poem for the occasion.

FOR ALISTAIR

Dear child, your godfather holds you with delight
and greets you with a prayer.
Why were you born? I wonder. Where, oh where
will your journey lead? How will you know
your destiny? I bless you with joy,
young pilgrim. Sheltered, protected now, soon you'll set out
on the great quest. Search bravely, little boy,
and don't forget you were born of love and joy.

Don't be afraid to ask questions
when it is time to do so. That's how you'll grow.
I pray that God in his mercy send
angels to guide you, leading you each day –
inspired teachers with words to satisfy
you when you're hungry; and when you thirst
water of life for your spirit; and when you're lost
life-giving comfort, a radiant Pentecost.

May tender compassion flower round you each day,
Alistair. May fruits of the Spirit – faith,
hope, humour, gentleness – be good companions.
In years to come, please pray for one who now
thanks God for you, commends you to God's love,
prays for your happiness, hugs you with delight,
rejoices with your parents, tries to sing
verses to celebrate your christening.

Pentecost
26th May 1996

The poem is undoubtedly inspired by one of Damian's favourite readings for many years which was the letter Dietrich Bonhoeffer wrote for his nephew on the occasion of his baptism (which, of course, he would be unable to attend) included in Bonhoeffer's *"Letters and Papers from Prison"* which begins *"This day you are born a Christian."* As has been already mentioned, when Damian was team teaching with Gerard Rummery in the National Pastoral Centre in Melbourne, Australia, in 1981, the two of them devised an audio-visual presentation for synchronised slide projectors of an abridged version of the Bonhoeffer text to the background of Respighi's *Ancient Airs and Dances.* Damian had a profound conviction about the importance of the sacraments as visible signs of the grace they conferred, as can be seen from two of his unpublished hymns in the appendix.

Among Damian's poems there are several which give an insight into his deep and loving concern for those whom he wished to help. Two such poems are given in the moving chapter entitled

Sharing the Darkness, which concludes the little book What's the Point of it all? treated elsewhere in this biography. This chapter was, as is mentioned elsewhere, to have formed part of the planned sequel to Growing into Faith. The poem, For Tony, which was introduced and read by Brother Gerard Rummery at Littlemore on the occasion of Damian's funeral, shows us how Damian's deep sensitivity and pastoral concern overflowed into a work of such intensity that it still has the power to unsettle and disturb.

TONY

Your eyes still haunt me, and your curling mouth
Armed with some question, smiling in disbelief.
I tried to help you, failed, and let you go –
I had to – but you never left my heart.
I often wonder what you're asking now.
(Still overturning someone else's apple cart?)
If, with that drugged intelligence you became
What you once promised – or just drifted on the stream

of your unconscious destiny: to doubt,
to keep on doubting. Your anxious father tried
To help, came to me by night, feared you'd find out.
That was the end, I think. And every word
Of those introspective questions, tortuous paragraphs
Of argument, half-baked views you'd read or heard,
Seemed all in vain. We never said goodbye.
I saw you wander away. That night I cried.

Other examples of Damian's songs, poems and hymns will appear later in the book. Perhaps here the reader is privileged to glimpse something of the depth of this most keenly sensitive man.

7 | Damian, the Practical Mystic

It may seem strange to some to speak of the jovial, fun loving Damian as a MYSTIC! But Chamber's Dictionary includes in its definition of the word the idea of someone special who see things *"hidden from the eyes of the ordinary person, only revealed to a spiritually enlightened mind."* PRACTICAL suggests that what was made known to the individual was not kept like the one talent buried in the ground, but applied to life. Taking the meaning of both words, therefore, two mediaeval mottos found their complementarity in him: *bonum est diffusum sui = goodness naturally shares itself*, and *aliis contemplata tradere = passing on to others what has been contemplated.* People who knew Damian remember him precisely not only because he saw with much greater insight into so many ordinary things but also because he freely shared with others what he had discovered. In that sense he was a practical mystic. His studies, his various experiences as teacher, leader of pastoral work, student, composer, author and writer, were all ultimately to the profit of those with whom he lived and worked. Because of this, it is difficult to isolate the formative influences in his life as though he simply became the person he was as the result of his formal education. He was eclectic by nature, open to all kinds of experiences in savouring things for the first time, always ready to learn from others but maintaining a critical balance in what he was taught and experienced.

All of this was not simply natural ability: the treasures which he shared so generously were accumulated through many years of study and hard work. For example, when he was preparing for his A levels, he was sent to the Brothers' house for students in Cambridge to spend some time with Brother Columban Cluderay, a great literary scholar and quite an exacting teacher. Damian occasionally recalled that the first piece of writing which he did for this enigmatic man was handed back to him with the observation, "I hope you can do better than this!" It certainly proved both a shock and a stimulus to Damian, as he would laughingly admit, and his next efforts won at least grunts of general approval from his mentor.

The fruits of his three years of undergraduate studies in Magdalene College, Cambridge, were gathered for the rest of his life by all those with whom he worked. He became, as has been already noted, a fine teacher of literature both in the Juniorate and at West Park Grammar School, St Helens, with an extraordinary ability to inspire and encourage his students. His later success in teaching and producing drama was developed through his years with the *Footlights* group in Cambridge. It was in these years that he cultivated his ability to read a text in such a way as to point the meaning, to bring out in the intonation and shading of his voice the nuances which he felt were contained in whatever he was reading: poetry was heard as poetry and the cadences of blank verse were exploited to show the inner coherence and meaning. Not much is known about other formative aspects of these years but two of his former fellow students in Magdalen in those years, Eamon Duffy and Nicholas Boyle, both now occupying academic posts in Cambridge, remember him for his wholehearted involvement in everything he took on.

It may have been one of his Cambridge teachers or tutors who first led him to see the importance of E.M. Forster's phrase, "*only connect!*" It became a motto for so many things which Damian did. As a teacher, organiser, reader, singer and liturgist, it was always his concern to work **with** others to help them appreciate whatever particular activity was going on. His teaching style was not that of the expert to whom everyone had to listen, but rather that of the leader, the cajoler inducing his audience to "connect", to see relevance. His style was that of dialogue. He worked through, questioning, receiving suggestions, building up from the group whatever he felt was needed so that the "connection" could be made. Brother Gerard Rummery gives an outstanding example of the way Damian could work with quite different audiences. In recalling the following incident:

> During his first visit to Australia in 1976, as part of our work in trying to bring some of the concerns of young people to the attention of the forthcoming Synod on Catechesis (1977), Damian had been invited to meet with a group of Year 12 students, girls and boys, from a number of Catholic schools in Adelaide. Up to this point most of our work had been with adults. The situation was not one we would have chosen: the young people brought together did not know one another, the meeting was to take place in a large hall, it was to be during the afternoon and the students were to be dismissed after the meeting. After we had talked about this for some time in Melbourne before leaving for Adelaide, Damian asked me to take him to the "biggest and best" music store. There, we sounded out the young assistant on what was the hottest album in town, the one most sought after by young people. It so happened that the group "Deep Purple" had just come out with a smash hit which just then was being released in Australia. We bought the tapes and were told that the hit would probably be one track called, if memory serves me correctly, "I've been misunderstood." We therefore contacted the organisers to make sure that they had a very powerful sound system and asked to have an assistant who could play things as Damian directed. In spite of all this preparation, I remember feeling distinctly uneasy as some 200 to 300 students, 16–17 year old girls and boys in various school uniforms, swarmed into the hall. Once a measure of silence had been obtained with some difficulty and the formalities of introduction were over, Damian was asked to take over. We had prepared three main questions and sub-questions which we had done out on a worksheet: Have you ever felt that you were misunderstood? By whom? Why did you feel this?

What did you do about it? What would you like to have done about it? An uneasy truce having been thus established while the audience worked at their sheets for some minutes, Damian had the lights in the hall dimmed and then, **at full volume,** had the particular track about being misunderstood played. The effect was extraordinary! The previous "what's all this about" attitude changed to something more serious. Groups were quickly formed, ideas were shared, some reporting was done, and then the track was played again. The second part of our questionnaire had asked: "Do you feel that you are understood by your church? If so, in what ways? If not, in what ways? This led to even more vigorous group discussion and finally to an open session of questions and answers in which Damian had the audience eating out of his hand. It was perhaps the most masterly display of making contact with young people which I was privileged to experience in his company. The afternoon session of some two hours ended up being almost too short for the richness of what was experienced. Not only was the applause at the end enthusiastic but the contrast between the mood of the young people at the beginning and the end was most striking. We often laughed over the supreme accolade given by three students who came to us at the end of the day and said something like this: "You two have got it right! **Deep Purple** is definitely it! Make sure the Pope [Paul VI] hears about it!"

It is worth reflecting on such an incident. At one level it can be read as an example of a gifted teacher knowing how to win over an audience. It certainly was that, but it was also someone helping these young people to "connect", to see the relationship between their faith and the events of life: faith, religion, church, being misunderstood, were all part of the one life, not separate from it.

Brothers Thomas, Benet and Damian, in their visit to St Aloysius, Highgate, had been asked to do the school assemblies for the week in which they were to work in the school. Damian drew the short straw and had to take the first one with Year 10 (4th Form). Benet takes up the story:

The Head of Year welcomed us (we were sitting right at the back of the hall) and then told the assembled crew that Damian would take the assembly. Not the most athletic of men, Damian made his way to the front, up the short stairs onto the stage and looked at them. He was carrying an open copy of the Daily Telegraph.

"Look what I've found! An amazing article on phobias. And we all know what a phobia is, don't we? An irrational fear over which we have no control. It says here that one in sixteen has a phobia." Then slowly looking round the hall said, "If there are 200 people here, that's a lot of phobias! I'll read out some of them." He went on to mention spiders, snakes, frogs, dogs and others. Then he focused on the top one of all. He looked at them with his eye-on-you gaze. "It says here that the top phobia of all is to be asked to say something in public without any preparation." Every boy in the room KNEW that Damian was going to ask them to say something! There was absolute silence. Damian resumed, saying that the article did in fact give hope and that it is possible to overcome phobias or at least control them. He didn't say he was not going to ask anyone to speak!

At this point the Head of Year came back into the hall. She'd been to see the Head about something. She opened the door and stepped in. She paused, astonished. Then she tip-toed to the front and said to the assembly in a whisper, "You can go now!" It was a masterpiece of crowd influence!

Damian then made his slow way to the back of the hall and sat down.

Another example of this ability of Damian's comes from his opening session in one of the *Vision and Vitality* programmes run by the Australian province for Brothers in the late 1980's. Many of Damian's friends will remember his masterly workshop on the man born blind in the 9th chapter of John's Gospel (cf. his chapter on the same theme in *What's the Point of it All?)* The participants in this session were mainly from Australia, Papua New Guinea and New Zealand, but there were some Brothers as well from parts of Asia. It so happened that one of the participants was Brother Ulrick Currie from Malaysia, an outstanding theological student who had taken his doctorate in Rome. Brother Ulrick had become blind in middle age. Damian was not aware of this at first but, having discovered Brother Ulrick's situation as he was conducting the workshop, adjusted things in such a way that Brother Ulrick was able to share the coming of blindness with the group. It was a moment not easily forgotten by all those present. At one level, there was the admiration of a group of teachers for a master teacher adapting his approach to his audience, but at another there was the feeling of a profound religious experience as Damian showed himself as the practical mystic, the servant of the Gospel read in the here and now of this particular group of believers.

Damian, because of all his teaching experience, was a participant in a three month session of the International Lasallian Centre at the begining of 1979 which was to look at young people today, particularly from the viewpoint of the kind of formation needed for those joining the De La Salle Brothers. There were about sixty Brothers of different nationalities from various parts of the world with three main languages being used: French, Spanish and English. All presentations were made in one of these languages with simultaneous translation into the other two.

The celebration of liturgy alternated between the language groups so that there was one celebration of the Eucharist in English for everyone once per week. Despite the challenge presented by the fact that the majority were not English speakers, Damian, very quickly accorded the role of natural leader of the English speakers, soon had all the members of this very diversified company singing enthusiastically from the first collection of *Songs of the Spirit,* from the refrains of *Walk in the Light* and *Bind us Together.* His influence radiated far beyond his own language group as the following tribute received from Frère Philippe de Montety, a long time missionary in Burkina Faso indicates:

> He (Damian) was an active tool for God's grace in me when I was in Rome for the CIL at the beginning of 1979. The simple statement of his experience was an encouragement to devote oneself to God: one could feel how God could work through him, using his gifts of music, of praise, and of warm friendship. You will not be surprised to hear that his songs are known and

used here. "O the word of my Lord" was sung at a perpetual profession in Nigeria, and a French version of it on a similar occasion in our community; and the French version of "Sing of a Girl" is a favourite with our "juvenistes (junior novices)"

Brother Louis Welker from Louisiana, who was a companion in the same programme with Damian and later served a stint in Kintbury, writes of him:

> The time I spent with him at CIL and at St Cassian's were precious hours that shall be treasured. Damian taught me so much about retreat work. In fact, just about everything I do with young people these days has its roots at St Cassian's. He was one of our bright lights who shall certainly be missed but never forgotten.

Damian always felt greatly enriched by his CIL experience. He often paid tribute to two French speaking Brothers who had a great influence on him through their presentations during the programme, Frères Michel Sauvage (France) and Maurice-Auguste (Belgium). From Michel, an outstanding theologian and Lasallian scholar, Damian felt that he had deepened his own biblical understanding of the history of salvation, in which each person is called to follow his particular *itineraire* or journey. From Maurice-Auguste, with whom he formed a deep friendship during his later work for the Rule Commission in Rome in 1984, he came to a deeper understanding and appreciation of Saint John Baptist de La Salle against the historical background of his time. From them both he treasured in, Michel Sauvage's phrase, his own discovery of the Founder of the Brothers, Saint John Baptist de La Salle, as *"the **man** who became a **saint**!"*

Another important 1979 CIL influence on Damian's subsequent work was the week presented by a French priest, Pierre Moitel, whom Gerard Rummery had met in 1975 in Paris in a national catechetical congress called *Catéchèse '80 (Catechesis for the '80's)* and invited to Rome to speak from his experience of the young people with whom he worked. Moitel's presentations, set in an historical framework which contrasted the view of the Church from the "inside" and from the "outside"as seen by young persons of today, insisted on the fundamental importance of what he called *"libérer la parole des jeunes"* or freeing young people to speak out as they saw things. It was something Damian had already learned and in which he believed strongly, but it was an important confirmation from such a compelling and credible witness. It also confirmed his growing interest in the catechetical movement generally and eventually was an important influence in leading him to feel the need for his subsequent theological studies and doctoral thesis.

This first long Roman experience introduced Damian to Italy, a country which he was to love and appreciate in subsequent activities as a member of an International Catechetical Commission of the De La Salle Brothers (1978–1981), a member of the Rule Commission (1983–1984) convoked to write the final version of the Brothers' Rule for presentation to the General Chapter of 1986, and as a presenter in a number of sessions of the International Lasallian Centre after 1986.

Undoubtedly one of the most important influences of this first stay in Italy was a week's retreat made by the whole CIL group in the month of March in an Assisi which was under snow. The retreat was organised chronologically around the story of Francis and Clare so that the Eucharist each evening was celebrated at an important place associated with the story of Francis's own vocation and that of the great family of which he was the founder. So, the sequence went from *San Damiano* to *Santa Chiara*, to *Santa Maria della Portiuncula*, to the *Carcere* or hermitage on Monte Subasio and finally to the tomb of Francis in the lower basilica after the cathedral had been closed for the night. Subsequent Kintbury groups were to become familiar with the Assisi Crucifix and with the wonderful ceramic chalices and patens of Mario Franchi, an Assisi potter whom Damian came to know, and whose ceramics he was later to offer as gifts to close friends. Besides deepening Damian's own knowledge and love for Francis, this first Assisi experience was to enrich the lives of so many others through Damian's discovery of two hymns, *Look at the Sky* (SS2,

179) and *Laudato Sii* (SS2, 189). This latter hymn was his adaptation of the words and music of an Italian hymn very popular with youth groups in Italy. The sentiments of the third verse were to resonate in his own later life, as Brother Nicholas Hutchinson has so finely pointed out in the dedication to his series *"Praying Each Day of the Year"*:

> Praise for those who spread forgiveness,
> those who share your peace with others,
> bearing trials and sickness bravely;
> *Even sister death won't harm them.*

Indeed, the following verse could also be read as a wonderful summary of Damian's own life, the practical mystic:

> For our life is but a song,
> and the reason for our singing
> is to praise you for the music;
> *join the dance of your creation.*

Some idea of the importance of Assisi for Damian can be gained by reading the fourth chapter of *What's the Point of it All?* in which Damian retells the story of the words spoken by the crucifix at San Damiano. In the section 'For Prayer and Reflection' Damian returns to the same theme:

> As a young man, Francis prayed constantly, 'Lord what do you want me to do?' You are invited to make the same prayer. Imagine that Jesus answers your prayer by saying (as he said to the blind man at Jericho) 'What do you want me to do for you? (Mark: 10:51). How do you reply?

Damian had a special love for the 11th chapter of the Letter to the Hebrews, a love which was strengthened when he discovered that it was also a favourite of Saint John Baptist de la Salle. In Damian's own adaptation of the *heroes of faith* in Alan Dale's paraphrase of this same Chapter 11, Damian adds some more characters: Mary at the Annunciation, Paul on the Damascus Road, Augustine heeding the children's song "take and read," and then Francis:

It (this action of God) illuminated for Francis of Assisi *a line of scripture which changed his life.*

In this first visit, in addition to Assisi, Damian was to visit other Italian cities, especially Perugia, Gubbio, Orvieto, Florence and Pompeii, all of which had their impact on him. His natural sense and appreciation of the dramatic was fired by his first viewing of the Caravaggio paintings of the calling, vocation and death of Saint Matthew in the church of *San Luigi dei Francesi* and the paintings of the *Conversion of Saul* and the *Death of Peter* in *Santa Maria del Popolo*. Having obtained the slides of these wonderful paintings, he was to share his discovery of them with many different audiences in subsequent years. This was the practical mystic sharing with others what he himself had discovered.

Damian's instinctive feel for the visual arts was yet another sign of his practical mysticism: important aesthetic and spiritual experiences were not moments which he hoarded for himself. Gerard Rummery recalls that one of his first memories of enjoying sculpture in Damian's company was when the two of them went to see the Arthur Dooley bronze statues of the *Stations of the Cross* at St Mary's, Leyland. Damian, very visibly moved by the juxtaposition of the starving Biafran child (it was the time of the civil war in Nigeria) in the composition of the group of persons surrounding the Crucifixion, went on his knees. In the visits which "Yes Week" groups from Kintbury made to Coventry Cathedral, Damian always highlighted the Jacob Epstein *Ecce Homo* in the ruins as well as delighting in showing these young people making their first visit to Coventry, John Piper's *Angels* etched in glass in the West Screen and the splendour of the great Baptism Window. He was later to make his own audio-visual from slides of Coventry Cathedral and use it towards the end of the "Yes Week" as a review of what the participants had encountered together. Indeed, he loved every aspect of Coventry, especially as the symbolism of combining the ruins and the modern structure appealed to his natural feel for the dramatic. But he made sure as well that all who came saw and felt the significance of the *"Father forgive…"* motif at the altar of reconciliation. In many excursions made later with Gerard Rummery during his various trips to Italy, Damian loved to return to some favourite places such as the lower basilica of Assisi and the cathedral at Orvieto precisely because these two close friends had a shared agreement that the principle of "deepening the familiar" in a book, a poem or a place was something qualitatively different from a completely new experience.

Damian's mystical side was also shown in his deep interest in music. Many who heard his party pieces ranging from Edith Piaf to pastiches of Gilbert and Sullivan (who could forget the *Hierarchy Song!*) to the Beatles may not have realised that the same Damian had a special interest in dramatic music such as that used by Wagner in the *Twilight of the Gods*. His initial interest probably came from his literary background and his study of the Siegfried legend at Cambridge but he was presumably attracted as well by the air of mysticism associated with the genre just as he was by the Arthurian legend and the romanticised story of Glastonbury. Indeed, he was to produce his own musical, *The Play of Siegfried*, as one of his first dramatic attempts while he was teaching in the Juniorate. It was the long musical phrases and Wagner's *leitmotif* technique which fascinated him so much that he twice attended all day performances of the complete *Twilight* when it was given in London. It was probably certain similarities of musical design which attracted him to the music of Elgar: works such as the *Cello Concerto*, the *Violin Concerto* and the splendid *Pomp and Circumstance* marches. A particularly dramatic experience of Elgar's *Dream of Gerontius* in late 1969 or early 1970 marked his life, as Gerard Rummery recalls:

> One memorable occasion of these years was our attending the Liverpool Philharmonic Hall for the final rehearsal of Elgar's "Dream of Gerontius" which Damian had never heard performed live. A staff member of West Park, Denis Lavelle, was in the Philharmonic Choir. The occasion was a very special

one – was it perhaps the centenary of the Liverpool Philharmonic? – which combined the forces of a Welsh Choir, a boys' choir, the Liverpool Philharmonic Choir and Orchestra, all under the direction of Charles Groves. The part of the priest was to be sung by a distinguished Liverpudlian, John Shirley-Quirk. It was already a sell-out concert so we accepted Denis Lavelle's invitation to attend the rehearsal. This in itself was extremely interesting as it was the first occasion when all these disparate groups came together. The never to be forgotten moment for both of us, however, was when John Shirley-Quirk, in casual clothes, arose and began the great Proficiscere Anima Cristiana – "Go forth, Christian soul!" which ends the first part of Gerontius. The strength of the voice, its exquisite modulation, filled the hall in such a way that everything else became subordinate, even though the three choirs were all singing at the same time. As the last notes died away there was a profound silence, followed by the orchestra members and all the choristers bursting into spontaneous applause – certainly an unusual event in rehearsals. The next evening we listened together to the radio broadcast from Liverpool but the performance never attained the same level as that rehearsal.

Damian often referred to these magical minutes and claimed that, in spite of seeking out various recordings of Gerontius, he had never found anything which came near to what we experienced that evening. The very nature of the oratorio led us to speak about dying and I recall this evening as the first of many occasions when we talked about death. I was still grieving from the unexpected death of one of my own brothers as it had not been possible to return for the funeral in Australia. Damian had already lost his mother and then he was to lose his stepmother. I can remember introducing him to a poem called "The Death of a Monk" by Lascelles Abercrombie, which tells of the surprise of a monk realising that he is dying all alone while he can hear the members of his community in the chapel reciting one of the Offices. The irony is in the very situation whereby any monk could normally expect to die surrounded by the members of the community while the Prayers for the Departing were recited. Damian himself was to die alone like this even though members of his community were nearby in the hospital at the time.

A practical mystic… Yes, so many letters and tributes received after his death spoke of the profound spiritual impact which Damian made through his many and extremely varied activities. For some, it was the insight which he brought to a scriptural text, for others it was the warm-hearted person with whom they had shared an Emmaus walk, for others it was the hospitable Damian of the kitchen or of the Kintbury entrance. Here are some typical letters, the first from one of his former students at St Helens:

> He was a teacher of RE and Drama when I was at West Park, St Helens, in the early seventies, and I particularly remember the fun we all had during the production of the plays that he directed. I equally remember vividly his approach in RE lessons, and I am grateful for the many progressive views he shared with us at the time, and for the fact that he made the church seem relevant.

Sister Ita remembers him in this way:

> At one time he did fill the room with his size, but he always filled it with his bubbling, energetic presence, his zest for life, for all that lives, his marvellous ease with words and music, the colour of all he was and did. This life was too limiting for him – his gaze started here but always went beyond to what we could become, to what we really are.

And Mark Condren, who himself served at Kintbury, writes of Damian's funeral Mass at Littlemore:

> The whole occasion was full of significance and deep reverence. I was touched deeply. Of particular significance was the number of people from all parts of the country who were able to attend… Looking around the reception room I saw my past – the very reason why I became a teacher. All those who had "touched my heart" were gathered. It was great to see them all. Indeed, it is probably only Damian who could have achieved it.

This final tribute comes from Joan Williams, an experienced headmistress, who became a close friend of Damian and a great supporter of Kintbury:

To witness the way in which Damian and his team, without heavy preaching or oppressive piety, infected youngsters with living faith is unforgettable. When disillusioned schoolgirls came to me for permission to hold 'a Kintbury type Mass' in their free time one Friday evening, I had plentiful proof that something important had happened to them.

What had happened? Damian's own goodness had touched the lives of others: what Damian himself had contemplated had been shared with others.

8 | The Post-Kintbury Years: Some glimpses

Damian spent a little over three months (January to April 1979) in Rome following the programme of the International Lasallian Centre. During this time he also took part in the first meeting of the International Catechetical Commission of the De La Salle Brothers to which he had been appointed. At this meeting Brother Gerard Rummery, who was on the staff of the International Centre, was appointed Secretary. The chairman of this commission was Brother Jeffrey Calligan from Louisiana, who, with Gerard, had been a member of the previous Commission 1972–1976. Jeffrey and Damian were already good friends as he and Gerard had presented a programme for teachers at Kintbury in 1976. During Damian's absence, Brothers Joseph and Dominic continued to run Kintbury with the help of the younger members of the team until Damian returned.

At the Catechetical Commission's meeting in April 1980, both Gerard and Jeffrey noticed that Damian arrived exhausted and spent most of the meeting battling a heavy cold. Gerard, having listened to Damian's account of his previous and forthcoming engagements, was so concerned that on April 15th 1980 he wrote to Brother Leander, Provincial, to express his own anxiety about the burden Damian was carrying.

> As someone who has been very close to Damian since I lived with him in St Helens in the early 1970's and during our

subsequent work together over the last ten years, I feel quite concerned about him at the moment and feel I should share these thoughts with you. I think he is feeling very keenly the burden of being "irreplaceable" at St Cassian's. A few years ago when he was in Australia, I think his very absence was one of the spurs which came to involve other people more deeply. Now, with Joe's future lying in another sphere (Brother Joseph Hendron was to become Novice Master) I think Damian has come to realise how much the success of recent years has depended on having other people who could take over and run programmes when he was away for some time. He feels that he cannot do this at present, much as he appreciates what is being done by... With the general uncertainty that these events pose, I detect considerable anxiety in Damian and am concerned that his complete involvement in his work could lead him to endanger his health (and his own efficiency) by trying to do too much... We both know the extraordinary qualities Damian brings to this work and it was seeing him arrive here exhausted that prompted me to write this letter.

Gerard's concern was not based simply on his close friendship with Damian. As a member of the St Helen's community in the winter of 1972, he had helped to carry Damian out from the community chapel one Saturday morning when he collapsed during the Mass. This took place at a time when Damian had been working frantically on one of his dramatic productions and had spent until midnight at rehearsals in the school at West Park. Damian insisted that he did not need to see a doctor but his subsequent medical history might have been different if he had agreed to a complete medical check-up after this incident. He insisted simply that the small community chapel had been too hot. After this collapse by Damian, the late Brother John O'Donnell, a fellow member of the community at the time, would, when he had to tell Damian that he was wanted on the phone, always mime or whisper, "Say No!" in an effort to get Damian to be more careful about the amount of work he took on.

As the Kintbury chronicle unfolded, Damian was able to be replaced at the end of 1982 and there has been ever since a succession of excellent leaders who have continued and developed the vision created by Damian, Joe and Dominic.

Damian himself had long felt the need to deepen his theological studies. He often spoke very highly of the personal debt which he felt he owed to Hubert Richards who, in a number of Kintbury sessions, had done so much to open up new and exciting Scripture scholarship for him and for so many others. After looking at a number of study possibilities, therefore, Damian enrolled in the graduate Bachelor of Divinity programme at Manchester University and moved to the Pendleton community. The Scripture studies of this graduate degree required Damian to learn New Testament Greek, a task he found difficult but to which he brought his usual energy with great success. It goes without saying that Damian plunged into this new and exciting world of study with great enthusiasm. One of his teachers, Reverend Ben Drewery, retired Senior Lecturer, wrote when he heard of Damian's death:

> He was (some years ago) one of my very best senior students in Early Church History and Doctrine and his own loyal Roman Catholicism and my own Methodism tended to enhance our mutual indebtedness: we found common ground in the tradition – and especially the theology and philosophy – of the early centuries.
>
> When he came back after his two years at the Vatican (Damian worked with the Rule Commission of his Institute in Rome from September 1984 to June 1985), he came here and we lunched together. No one was more popular or highly thought of.

Damian's course work was of the highest standard – his papers and thesis were all graded at top level – so it was a disappointment within the Faculty that his physical inability to answer more than four of the five required questions during the time allocated for the three hour written examination cost him the first-class degree which his work merited. Those who remember his very individual handwriting will recall that he always wrote slowly. He was told afterwards by one of his professors that if he had offered even a summary of what he had intended to write for his fifth answer, he would have been awarded at least a 1.2. But when he was asked by the Faculty if there were any extenuating circumstances which he wished to be taken into consideration, Damian simply remarked that at forty years of age he was no longer capable of accelerating what had become his own very individual style of handwriting.

The fact that Damian had these two years of study might give the impression that he gave up other activities during this time. Nothing could be farther from the truth! He was still involved with Lasallian Resource, collecting and writing hymns for *Songs of the Spirit 3* which appeared in 1985, and he continued to be involved with some of the "Yes Weeks" and other Kintbury Conferences.

Rule Commission, Rome 1984–1985

The De La Salle Brothers, founded in 1680 in France, had become a worldwide Institute which, since 1956, had endeavoured to re-express itself through a Rule of life which took more account of this international identity. A working version of the Rule had been authorised in 1967 for an experimental period of 20 years so that, as the General Chapter of the Institute of 1986 approached, it was necessary to convoke a group of experts and scholars of different nationalities to propose a final form of the Rule for the approval of this Chapter. The task would require the members of this Commission to reside in Rome from September 1984 to the end of June 1985. Damian was asked to serve on this Commission as one of the two native English speakers along with Brother Luke Salm, a theologian from Manhattan College, New York, USA. The other members of the Commission came from different countries and Damian was particularly pleased to be working with Brother Maurice-Auguste, a Belgian, one of the great scholars of his Institute, whose presentations had meant so much to him during his time in CIL in 1979.

This was a very important year in Damian's life. First of all, the nature of the work was such that it imposed a much more balanced and regular style of life on him. The work was demanding - meetings morning and afternoons every day - and the fact that the task was carried out in French exacted its own price from Damian, whose French, though competent from his time in CIL and from his work in the International Catechetical Commission, had not previously been taken formally beyond O-level. The benefits of this deeper knowledge of French were reaped in certain aspects of his later doctoral studies, especially in the second chapter of his thesis where his reading in French journals and books gave him a very detailed knowledge and understanding of the important catechetical movement in France in the post war period. The more structured life in Rome, following his two years of study, offered Damian continued scope for wide reading. He himself would acknowledge the great value of the sustained work in French on a Rule which, for all its necessary precision of thought and expression in French, had to find adequate expression as well in other languages, including of course the many varieties of English represented in the 83 countries of the Institute. A second point of great importance was that Damian found himself living these nine months in Rome with some of the most intellectually gifted members of his Institute, close to the concerns of the Church and his own General Council, and in regular contact with Gerard Rummery as they planned future work together. Much of the breadth and richness of the last ten years of Damian's life flowed from this "sabbatical" year. It is indeed during this period that Damian finally wrote the four articles on the origin and development of Kintbury for the Institute's journal called *Lasalliana*, a project which he had had in mind for many years.

Damian and controversy

The public controversy which later erupted over *Weaving the Web*, the programme on which Damian worked with other members of the National Project after 1988, was keenly felt by Damian but it was by no means the first time in which his whole approach to developing the faith of young people had been criticised by others who took a more traditional viewpoint. Indeed, one way of interpreting Damian's choice of a theme for his doctoral studies would be his reflection on his own experience of the difficulties which he had experienced with adults who were uncomfortable or downright opposed to his way of working with young people. While the conflict at one level was probably inter-generational, there was much else to take into account since this was a something taking place all around the world even if the manifestation of this conflict took different forms in different cultures. The history of Catholics in the British Isles, centuries in which the Roman Catholic faith as such had to be defended from various forms of persecution, had certainly tended to make many Catholics more inward than outward looking. Teachers and youth ministers, were often the persons who became more immediately aware of the deep faith questions which young people have asked more and more in modern societies. This often meant that teachers, catechists and youth workers, appear to some parents and other adults to be too much on the side of the young people. While the controversies so aroused are portrayed as theological differences, the reality is both more complex and more subtle. The adults cannot see the world as their children see it and they too easily blame others for "disturbing the faith" of their children when the teacher or catechist has met young people at the level where they are already questioning so many aspects of life and faith. Most teachers of religion in recent years have experienced this tension with parents and, often with clergy, who are themselves often caught between the varying expectations of the traditions of the past and the demands of the present.

The long years of defending the faith are an important part of the Catholic heritage. The momentous changes initiated by the Second Vatican Council, the vernacular replacing the "blessed mutter of the Mass" in Latin, the re-appropriation of many Christian hymns which were considered 'Anglican' or 'Presbyterian' or 'Protestant' when they were often English translations of some of the oldest Latin hymns, the introduction of guitars into forms of liturgy and para-liturgy etc. appeared vaguely threatening and more easily resisted than adopted. This is not surprising since the history of the Second Vatican Council 1962–1965 shows the wide divergence of opinions held by the Council Fathers themselves. The fact that the initial working documents of the Council were transformed through prolonged debates and discussions shows that the Church's own taking stock of itself did not happen without deep and, in a few instances, permanently divisive controversy. The Council's great vision for the Church had to be put into action at parish level. And it was here, in implementing some of these changes, that Damian's own deep understanding of liturgy, allied with his closeness to young people, contributed so much to the success of Kintbury. Liturgical celebration was only one aspect of the Kintbury experience but it was often the one which seemed to leave the greatest impression on the young people who participated. Not that everyone saw it that way, as Joan Williams recalls:

> Some of my staff were a bit critical of Kintbury – that was until I told them a thing or two! The "Kintbury experience" (which anyway they had never seen) might not have been the cup of tea of middle-aged ladies with somewhat conventional views, but for young people it was **perfect.** Girls who were fed up with the Church, and particularly with "old Fr So-and-so" came home with the new and surprising discovery that Christianity was loving, open, generous and **joyful.**

Gerard Rummery recalls a particular example of how Damian's conviction that liturgical changes mandated by the Church were important, resulted in a change being introduced at one St Helens parish in 1970 in a most unexpected way. Newly arrived from Australia and from a renewal session in Rome, Gerard had expressed some surprise to find that there was no Exchange of Peace in the parish church which the Brothers' community attended. As the fairly elderly parish priest celebrated Mass for the Brothers on Saturday mornings in the community chapel, Damian took advantage of the parish priest's presence at breakfast to ask Gerard across the breakfast table whether or not the sign of peace was exchanged in other places where he had been. Gerard takes up the story:

The question, of course, was not completely innocent. Damian, as a member of the parish council, had already proposed on a number of occasions that the sign of peace be adopted in the parish. The parish priest, therefore, replied that 'the people do not want it.' Damian suggested that they should at least be consulted. The parish priest added that, to his way of thinking, there was a fundamental objection: the sign of peace was not British! Damian retaliated that, British or not, it was certainly Christian. The parish priest, then, said that he would prove conclusively to us all that the sign of peace was not wanted by having it implemented the following morning at the Sunday Mass which the Brothers attended. The following morning, therefore, the announcement was made before Mass that 'today we'll have the sign of peace when I tell you.' The moment having arrived, the parish priest wished peace to the congregation and then asked them to give a sign of peace to one another. As most parishioners had never experienced this beforehand, there was a certain hesitation, even confusion. Seeing this confusion the parish priest, shouting 'I'll show you what to do', advanced towards a small altar boy who, seeing a hand coming towards him at head level, ducked! The response of the congregation through spontaneous laughter resulted in a most cordial exchange of peace taking place and becoming established thereafter!

During the three months in 1977 in which Damian and Gerard worked together in some 11 different dioceses and Pastoral Centres of Australia and New Zealand, they frequently encountered opposition to their presentations from a traditionalist group in the English speaking world called CUFF (Catholics United For the Faith) and some other like-minded individuals and or groups.

This conflict was inevitable. The particular emphasis of their work together was to document the concerns of young people, so that these concerns could be submitted to the 1977 October Synod on Catechesis in Rome by some of the bishop-delegates. In each centre where they worked with young people, therefore, Damian and Gerard usually invited them, as individuals or as groups, to write a personal letter to Pope Paul VI expressing their concerns and hopes for the Church as they saw it. Many of these letters were shared with the adult groups with whom they worked and proved the basis for some very stimulating exchanges and for very important growth in appreciation of what some young people felt about the Church.

This was not the case, however, with everyone whom they met. Already Damian and Gerard were emphasising the importance of allowing space and time for young people to make explicit the gift of faith which they had received at their Baptism. Much of the emphasis which later found expression in the title of their book *Growing into Faith* grew out of these three months together where the unexpected preposition in the title was a deliberate attempt to express more graphically the dynamic aspect of faith:

> To grow **into** faith – not to 'keep' or protect the faith already received, but to grow gradually into faith – is for many Catholics an unfamiliar and challenging way of thinking. To grow into faith implies becoming more open to God, more receptive to his word, more responsive to his call, more faithful to his service. We are asked not so much to defend or protect the faith we have already received (as if it is a 'thing', say a body of beliefs, inside us) but to develop attitudes of honest searching, sensitivity to God's word, and concern for others – to become a good traveller, ready to trust and to endure, prepared to make the journey of a lifetime.

During their three months on the road in 1977, Damian and Gerard ran into a certain amount of organised opposition. They tried to develop a method which invited open dialogue by putting before their audiences the same challenges which they themselves had encountered in the setting up of their workshops. To help them do this, they tried to turn the opposition which they encountered into a positive educational experience for all concerned. One of the most successful methods which they devised together was one referred to as the *Seven Statements*, in which seven very contrasting statements on the same topic were read out to the participating group. This was a kind of game in which participants were given a prepared answer sheet which consisted of a kind of chart, divided into two columns headed as Statement A and Statement B, with two other columns at the side with the title A Points or B Points. There were seven topics, each one having an A statement and a B statement. Damian read one, while Gerard the other. The contrast was not only in the content. Damian tended to read his statements in a most authoritative way while Gerard read his in a rather more easy-going manner. There were 5 points to be allocated for the statements heard but the rules were such that the participants could allocate 5 to one statement and zero to the other, 4 points to one statement and 1 to the other, or 1 to one and 4 to the other but **not** 3 and 2 or 2 and 3! The rules, in other words, forced the players to take a strong position with regard to the Statements: they could not simply sit on the fence. At the end of the game, the players were asked to add up their points to see whether they had more points in the A column or the B column. There was no public revelation of what individuals had scored but simply a direction to indicate whether their personal allocation of points included more in A than in B. All of this was usually carried out without any problem. But then the participants always asked: *Where do these statements come from?* At this stage, the audience would be told that all the A statements were taken from the Letter columns of various Catholic papers while the B statements were from the letters written by young people to Pope Paul VI to indicate what they saw as important issues for the forthcoming Synod. Copies of the Statements, indicating the origin of each, were then distributed to everyone in the group. This always resulted in a very animated discussion.

In most cases, this proved to be an excellent way of launching the various workshops, all of which had the title *The Church and Young People*, because it clearly demonstrated the important differences in perception by adults and young people of the same issues. There was one instance, however, when a small number of participants felt that they had been "manipulated" because they had not been told about the origin of these statements from the beginning. Because of this, they refused to stay for the rest of the workshop. This was unfortunate but it certainly showed that different positions could be adopted with regard to the same material.

In another instance, Damian had happened to narrate (in his own inimitable way) the story already mentioned above, of how the exchange of peace came to be adopted by the parish in St Helens. It was with some surprise, therefore, that a bishop in whose diocese Damian and Gerard had worked, at his invitation and to his great satisfaction, later let the two Brothers know of a letter of complaint which alleged that *"Brother Lundy is going around making fun of our elderly and hard working clergy!"*. One of the most delightful examples of this resistance to change, often recalled by Damian, was the questioner who demanded with some degree of indignation, *"Why do we have to change the way of saying the Our Father? Can't we say it in Latin as Jesus taught it to us?"*

One of the continuing points of controversy with some persons in Damian's Kintbury years, and in the subsequent history of Kintbury, was the celebration of liturgy. The Kintbury surroundings were less formal and the Mass could be prolonged in a way which was not possible in an ordinary parish. The young people following the session were, probably for the first time in their lives, actively involved in the preparation of the liturgy. They were asked to deepen the sense of the Readings through the music which they were invited to choose. They were encouraged to formulate some of the Prayers of the Faithful. Readers were required to prepare what they read so that the message was clear to all those who listened. All of this helped to create a certain *ownership*, an understanding of the celebration of Eucharist in a way which they had not previously known. This, not surprisingly, sometimes led young people after their Kintbury experience, as Brother Dominic Green remembers so many of them saying, to complain of the way in which they found their own parish Mass, *"dead boring!"*

One such complaint about the liturgy in Kintbury in 1982, sent to Brother Leander, the Provincial Superior of the De La Salle Brothers in Britain, stated that some young people *"come back to their parishes with some avant-garde ideas of the liturgy, for example substituting a non-biblical reading for one of the Scripture ones."* Brother Leander, writing directly to Bishop Emery of Portsmouth, defended Kintbury quite vigorously, pointing out that the complaints were unfounded and had never been forwarded directly to the persons responsible for the Kintbury Centre. He continued:

> The style of liturgy celebrated at St Cassian's is especially suited to young people who visit the Centre from all parts of the country in large groups, usually at their own expense, as Bishop David Konstant emphasized when he addressed the CRMS (Meeting of Religious Superiors) at Westminster last September, where St Cassian's was offered as a model of what the religious orders can do to help the Church develop new and more effective forms of youth ministry. The concerns voiced over and over again at St Cassian's reveal the unfortunate state of the liturgy in a large number of parish churches where the principles of the Vatican II Constitution and "General Instruction" are sadly not understood or not applied, with the consequent disillusionment and boredom of young people, many of whom drift away from the Church while others opt out more decisively…

> The style of liturgy developed at St Cassian's may not be to everyone's personal taste, but that does not call its orthodoxy into question: it involves plenty of lively singing, a more relaxed and friendly sign of peace than is usually offered in our churches, a greater level of spontaneous prayer, and a generally less formal atmosphere than that which prevails in our parish churches.

The correspondence on this issue is interesting from a number of points of view because at the same time as Damian and Kintbury were being attacked, the head of the diocesan liturgy commission was not only inviting Damian to spend two days working with the members but was also suggesting to them that they should take the opportunity to visit Kintbury and experience the liturgy as it was being celebrated there with young people.

It is not surprising, therefore, that when Damian was offered the opportunity to continue doctoral studies, it was his own experience of the difficulty of change in the Church which preoccupied him and became the focus of his work

Damian's Doctoral Thesis: "Adult Catechesis in the Roman Catholic Church in Britain since the Second Vatican Council"

It was towards the end of his Roman sojourn 1984–1985 that Damian was in touch by letter with Brother Joseph Hendron, who had just assumed the role of Provincial. As he concluded his work in Rome, Damian was wondering what his future work would be and had written to Brother Joseph to see if he had anything particular in mind. In a letter written from Rome on May 16th 1985, Damian reflects on the answer he received from his Provincial in answer to his own.

It was good to hear from you and thanks especially for thinking aloud about different points which show how uncertain the whole situation is and how many problems remain to be resolved before I can be assigned to some specific new job. I am glad you feel I should continue some writing and research…

I'd like to open up another possibility here, asking you to think about it and perhaps to give me a ring if you think that would help. One thing I had considered doing was asking to look out for and apply for a suitable job in tertiary education or adult work (catechetics, renewal)… I know that if I am to get anywhere at all in tertiary education I shall need to do a higher degree – a doctorate. As you know, I had hoped to do this part-time while working at Hopwood. I am keen to be pastorally involved, yet I have to accept that somewhere along the road, two or three years of pretty hard slog await! And I do have mixed feelings about that, as you can guess!

I hope you know that I am ready to be of service in whatever way you think is best and that it is far from my mind, in trying to find out where I go from here, to seek any special favours. If I do doctoral work, I'll certainly want to continue some form or forms of pastoral involvement on a part-time basis, say in retreat work or catechetics…

It is worth commenting on this last paragraph of Damian's letter. The particular form of consecration made by the Brothers includes the radical formula: *I promise to go wherever I may be sent and to do whatever I may be assigned by the body of the Society or its superiors.* Damian's letter shows that this formula was taken seriously by him. Although he and Brother Joseph had worked so closely together for so many years, Damian was not asking for any special privileges because of that.

Subsequent correspondence with Brother Joseph shows that Damian would be accepted at Manchester University as a doctoral candidate provided that his professor received a statement from his Provincial indicating that he would be free to work for at least three days a week on the doctorate during the next two to three years. In a letter of 5th June 1985, Professor A.O. Dyson of the Faculty of Theology wrote to Damian indicating that he would present Damian's application personally as the time for enrolling was already past.

> I would write a supportive letter to the PhD Committee of Senate, pointing out the class and quality of your first degree at Cambridge, the fact of your having held a post in higher education, the highly successful completion of the BD, which is a postgraduate degree, including a thesis which achieved a first class mark...

It was in this way that Damian returned to the Pendleton community in which he had previously lived, and launched himself into his doctoral studies. It is sometimes necessary to be reminded of this because Damian seemed to have done so much pastoral work in the next three years from September 1985 to October 1988 that it is difficult to imagine where he found the time to study.

But study he did and his doctoral thesis, some aspects of which will now be considered, is a most impressive work which is still waiting to be exploited by other researchers. In its third, fourth and fifth chapters, it offers an unparalleled detailed study on the post-Vatican Council history of the Catholic Church in England from the point of view of adult education. The Church in Britain, and indeed in the English speaking world, is all the poorer that Damian's last years of uncertain health precluded the preparation of the book (based on the thesis) which he had always intended to write.

Scope of the thesis

In his first outline of his projected thesis in October 1985, Damian tentatively sees the subject as *"Adult catechesis in the Roman Catholic church in Britain from 1959 to 1985, in relation to the Second Vatican Council."* The starting point for him, therefore, was an overview of the Vatican Council especially from the viewpoint of its sixteen final documents inasmuch as they created the need for understanding, absorption and acceptance by church members – a massive programme in itself – and hence a process which gave great importance to adult education. But, as can easily be imagined, Damian had first to look back on the history of the church in Britain following the restoration of the hierarchy in 1850. An important part of his preliminary study, therefore, concentrates on those aspects of the Modernist crisis which affected the English church, especially those concerning the condemnation of Tyrell. Indeed, Damian became so fascinated by his study of this period, that he had to recognise that this was not the main focus of his work. It did however proove helpful in discerning the bases of the conflict which is always present between the old and the new, the traditional expression and the insights of modern scholarship.

This chapter, the beginning of his research, becomes a chapter of some 100 pages in the final version of the thesis after a judicious pruning. In a letter to Gerard Rummery of 19th February 1987, Damian says," *Chapter 1 on Vatican II went down well with Professor Dyson and is on ice for a year, prior to having its 200 pages reduced by half! It's slow work, as you well appreciate."*

From a pastoral point of view, Damian's research found its practical expression through the book, written with Dom

Christopher Jamieson and Sister Louisa Poole, called *"To Live is to Change."*

Damian set out the scope of the thesis which he wished to develop in the following words:

> I want to examine the theological issues behind various conflicts in the church between practitioners of adult catechesis and the church's teaching authority. I chose this topic because I felt the whole area needs research and is of urgent pastoral importance. I am keen to make a solid academic contribution to the debate and praxis within the church.

It is worth pointing out that Damian's concern, as expressed in this outline, is not solely intellectual. Indeed, the spur is undoubtedly his own long experience of controversy but he underlines the *"urgent pastoral importance"* and the need for a solid *"academic contribution"* not only to the theory but also to the *praxis*, that is to what is actually being done in the church. Later in the same outline he contrasts two statements from church documents, one from 1965 which speaks of catechetical instruction being carefully imparted *"not only to children and adolescents, but also to young people and even to adults"*, and a document of 1971 which states that Pastors *"should bear in mind... that the catechesis of adults, since it has to do with people who are capable of fully responsible commitment, must be accepted as the principal kind of catechesis, towards which all other forms .. are directed."* What he calls *"the enormous distance which has been travelled between these two statements"* leads Damian to see the need for a study of the catechetical movement before and after Vatican II. This becomes the second chapter of his work, summed up in the title which he borrows from a seminal article by André Liégé, *"From catechism to catechesis."*

By April 1986, Damian's report on his research shows him immersed in the history of the post 1945 catechetical movement, especially in the documentation in French. Towards the end of the research outline he is beginning to refine his perceptions and see some of the ways in which the Vatican Council and the catechetical movement both faced the same basic problem as it is outlined in an article by John W. O'Malley:

> Aggiornamento (being up to date) proved to be more dynamic and uncontrollable than either Pope John or the Council intended, leaving us with the still unresolved problem of 'How is the present to deal with the past, and what legitimate hold does the past have on the present?'

Damian then continues,

> I suggest that this is the fundamental question underlying the bitter disputes in the catechetical world after the Council, including the problems in the English church's attempt to move forward.

By late December 1987 Damian had written more than 180 pages on his analysis of the movement from catechism to catechesis. In the first days of January 1988, Gerard passed through London and was able to read the chapter and make his own comments on it, just as Damian had done for Gerard's thesis in St Helens in 1972. Damian writes to Gerard on 5th January saying *"Thanks very much for reading through my second chapter and for the helpful suggestions you offered, which I shall follow up when I get Ch.5 out of the way."*

The third chapter of Damian's thesis is a detailed study of the foundation, development and closure of Corpus Christi College, London. This was a catechetical centre founded in 1965 by the English Bishops' Conference under the leadership of Cardinal Heenan, Archbishop of Westminster, who entrusted the guidance of the college to Hubert Richards, a well known and respected Scripture scholar, and a specially selected team. The college offered a post graduate course affording English speakers a similar kind of education to that being offered by the well established training schools for catechists operating in Brussels (Lumen Vitae) and in France. Damian, with the help of personal correspondence afforded by Hubert Richards who had been invited to direct a number of Kintbury workshops, traces the history of the college, its recognition as an outstanding centre of adult formation, the long drawn out controversy surrounding it, and its eventual closure in 1975.

In a letter to Gerard Rummery of 13th May 1988, Damian gives another update on his research and his writing.

> All's going well with the research. Recently I spent some days in the British Museum Library reading the entire Sower (an important and influential catechetical magazine founded by Canon Drinkwater) from 1915–1975. Fascinating and engrossing! I'm writing up the Corpus Christi affair at the moment. My verdict: tragic but inevitable. As Bert Richards wrote in 1972: 'Those who are fond of describing the church as the Body of Christ should not forget what happened to that body!'

It was this chapter on Corpus Christi which Damian had wished to expand into a book. Although the thesis chapter is around 100 pages the original version was much longer and, naturally, some of the more anecdotal material did not retain its place in an academic thesis. But the issues raised by the whole story presented on a national stage the kind of controversy which continues to present great difficulties for those who work in pastoral programmes with young people and with adults. In some ways, Damian's concern to set out the history of Corpus Christi as a case study with practical implications for the church anticipated what he and those associated with the National Project would subsequently suffer over the *Weaving the Web* controversy.

In the fourth chapter of his thesis Damian takes up the history of the National Pastoral Congress of 1980, an important event for the church in England which has been the subject of a number of studies. Damian saw the groundswell towards the Congress in the following terms:

> The Congress happened as the result of a conviction that a new pastoral strategy was needed within the Catholic Church in England and Wales. As an experience of consultation, it was fundamentally different from what a small working party of

experts would have been, perhaps less effective in a practical way, but it was a valuable inspirational and educational experience for delegates and for the larger church.

The Congress document, called *The Easter People*, marked an important step forward for the church in England and Wales, even if a number of commentators have subsequently felt that in trying to address a number of different audiences it may not have really satisfied any one of them. Damian's own evaluation, based on his analysis of the Modernist conflict in England in the earlier part of his thesis, is that it did indeed mark an important step forward at a national level even if experience tends to show that implementation of pastoral reform has to begin at the local level.

The final chapter of Damian's thesis is a detailed examination of the *Rite of Christian Initiation of Adults* as a model for adult catechesis in the Catholic church. While he shows that the seeds of this development can be traced to conciliar texts, he also shows that it was the practical experience of the French church before the Vatican Council which probably carried more weight in the subsequent development of RCIA.

What is interesting (and of course typical) about Damian's research on this chapter is that, having examined the development of the RCIA programmes in the English speaking world in general and in Britain in particular through the available literature, he then spent time working with an experienced practitioner, Sister Céline, who was engaged in trying to introduce the RCIA into various parishes of the diocese of Middlesborough. Damian's practical experience of this kind constantly illuminates his evaluation of the RCIA in terms of its content and process.

In October 1987, while he was still in the throes of finishing his thesis, Damian was approached by Bishop David Konstant, Chairman of the Department for Christian Doctrine and Formation, inviting him to work as a full-time member of the team responsible for the National Project of Catechesis and Religious Education, called *Living and Sharing Our Faith*. The minutes of this meeting indicate the qualities looked for in such a person and end by stating that the *"overall first choice"* among the names suggested was that of Damian Lundy.

Damian proposed this to the Council of his Institute in the following words:

> I would like to accept this job, since I see it as an opportunity to make a valuable contribution to the Church, and to use the fruits of my pastoral experience and academic research... I would not be available to take up the job until the end of October 1988, since I am due to present my thesis earlier that month. I have every hope of completing my research by then and of submitting the thesis on time.

Damian was authorised to accept the position, something which gave him great satisfaction as he wrote to Gerard on 14th December 1987:

> I have been offered and accepted an excellent job: in the National Office in London (although I don't need to live in London) working on the national project on Catechesis and Rel.Ed. – writing, researching, leading study days, animating, etc. It sounds very good, and I'll enjoy working with Jim Gallagher.

9 | # Damian and the National Project

So here was his chance to work with Jim on the National Project Committee. The work on the project had been going on for some time, its initiation having been undertaken by Fr Paddy Purnell, a Jesuit, assisted by Fr Jim Gallagher, a Salesian. When Fr Purnell moved on from the project, Fr Gallagher took over as its co-ordinator; much of what follows is his reflection on how it progressed. Under his guidance, the project took on a much broader dimension than was first envisaged by the Bishops' Conference and NBRIA (National Board of Religious Inspectors and Advisors), growing from a Primary school focus to becoming a whole-community project. In the August-September 1991 edition of *Priests and People*, Fr Gallagher, now co-ordinator of the National Project of Catechesis and Religious Education, wrote a fascinating and enlightening article. It provides background into why Damian was invited to become part of it.

Living and Sharing our Faith: a National Project

Next year, in Low Week 1992 to be precise, *The National Project of Catechesis and Religious Education* will be ten years old. That may come as news to some readers: news not only that the Project is nearly ten years old, but news that there is such a thing as a National Project. Others, particularly readers of the letters in *The Universe*, may have some idea of its existence but identify it with *Weaving the Web*, the RE resources for the first three years of secondary school. If they accept the opinions of the majority of letters published in the paper, they no doubt condemn it and hope that that is the end of it. Others may think it is all about some RE programme for our primary schools which is taking a very long time to appear. There is, of course, more to the National Project of Catechesis and Religious Education than the provision of RE resources for our primary and secondary schools.

The Project did begin with the decision to revise the RE programme for Catholic primary schools in England and Wales. In 1982 most dioceses were using the Irish catechetical programme, the *Children of God* series published by *Veritas*. Many diocesan advisers and teachers were of the opinion that, despite its excellent qualities, the Irish programme was not entirely suited to the different social, cultural and religious situations to be found in England and Wales. The National Board of Religious Inspectors and Advisers reported to the bishops that they thought it was time, to undertake a very thorough revision or to produce a home-grown programme for our primary children. In their Low Week meeting the bishops decided that such a work was necessary 'in order to be in tune with the multicultural and multi-faith background of our people'.

It was not long before those responsible came to the conclusion that a totally new venture was needed. For too long we had borrowed and adapted programmes which came out of and addressed different pastoral and educational needs. *The General Catechetical Directory* (1971) had urged that each region provide its own programmes. The Directory set out guidelines for drawing them up. Eleven years later we set about the task. The original title for the 'new venture' was *PREP: The Primary Religious Education Programme*. It was also thought wise to consider the needs of children up to the age of 14. After that age a different approach was thought to be necessary for a more questioning stage of maturity. A contract was drawn up with Collins for the publication of these RE resources.

Fr Patrick Purnell SJ, then the National Adviser for Religious Education, set the work in motion in liaison with diocesan advisers. It was thought necessary to consider the religious education of our children in the light of the documents of Vatican II and recent Roman and national texts which dealt with catechesis as the process of educating to and in the faith. It was evident that these texts would have to be carefully studied and practical implications for a primary school programme worked out in the light of them.

All of these texts stress that catechesis involves a process of growth in faith which is gradual and life-long; it is seen as a journey which comprises various stages. Each journey, however, is unique since those on the pilgrimage of faith start from different experiences and travel at their own pace. Adult catechesis is seen as central, 'the principal form of catechesis', because 'it is addressed to persons who have the greatest responsibilities and the capacity to live the Christian message in its fully-developed form'.

The texts also speak of some key dimensions of catechesis. These are briefly summarised in the national directory, *Sharing the Light of Faith*, issued by the bishops of the United States of America in 1979: 'its [catechesis] components include sharing, faith life, experiencing liturgical worship, taking part in Christian service and participating in religious instruction' (no.39).

Another factor which is strongly emphasised in the texts is the role of the whole Christian community: we are all responsible for catechesis. It is not a task which can be left to one or two in the community – teachers or catechists. This feature of catechesis is at the heart of the RCIA: 'the initiation of catechumens takes place step by step in the midst of the community of the faithful' (Introduction, 19). The bishops in the 1977 Synod declared that 'the model for all catechesis is the baptismal catechumenate'.

The introduction to the rite of baptism for children stresses this point: 'The people of God, that is the Church, made present in the local community, has an important part to play in the baptism of both children and adults. Before and after the celebration of the sacrament, the child has the right to the love and help of the community' (no.4).

In the catechesis of children and the young this community element calls for partnership between home, parish and school and a recognition of their complementary, distinct tasks.[4] The school is one partner. It cannot be held responsible for the whole task of educating, to and in the faith. RE lessons are only part of what the school has to offer. The school setting and atmosphere should be permeated by the Gospel spirit of freedom and love and present an array of values which are actually lived.

In the light of directions set out in these documents, it was argued that *PREP* should broaden its scope. Rather than simply re-edit a primary school programme to meet the particular needs of England and Wales, it should re-focus attention on the community of faith in which our children are being religiously educated. It should seek to provide guidelines and practical resources which would be suited to the needs of adults and children in different situations and in the variety of settings in which catechesis and religious education take place.

It was at this time that the title was changed. In place of *PREP* it now became *Living and Sharing Our Faith: a National Project of Catechesis and Religious Education*. This book takes up the fact that we are concerned with a life-long process which involves us all, adults and children, teachers, catechists, priests and grandparents. Catechesis is not the prerogative of experts. These are needed to enable and encourage all of us to find the confidence to do the task which is properly ours. To call it 'a project of catechesis and religious education' is to accept the fine distinction and overlap between these two tasks. To give RE lessons to twenty-five children from a variety of religious backgrounds and experiences is not quite the same task as working with children or adults who seek to deepen an already existing Christian faith, however initial it may be. This point is clearly made in the latest Vatican document on *The Religious Dimensions of Education in A Catholic School* (66–73).

Project publications of the last nine years provide resources for catechesis in the home, parish and school as well as RE programmes for schools. Others are being prepared. The structures and consultation process of the Project are rather complicated. Project texts are published with the authority of the Department of Catholic Education and Formation, the Bishops' Conference of England and Wales. They are born out of the expertise and experience of people working in catechesis and religious education. They are enriched by the comments of those who take part in the consultation process. Finally they are offered to the Catholic community not as the definitive word but as help and encouragement in the task of siving and sharing our faith in England and Wales today.

For me personally, and for others, this process has been keenly sensed and experienced particularly in the preparation for the primary RE programme which has been going on for two years now. Way back in 1982 we set out to re-edit a primary programme. At that time the bishops' suggested that it might take to the end of the decade to produce. We are not far off target. Meantime, many useful resources have been produced. The new primary programme is to be seen and judged in the wider Project context of living and sharing our faith.

It was precisely at the point when the programme was broadened to become *Living and Sharing Our Faith: a National Project of Catechesis and Religious Education* that Damian was co-opted onto the committee. He was, effectively, head hunted.

Jim was now the co-ordinator since Fr Purnell had moved on. Jim had known Damian for many years for they were contemporary Heads of RE, Jim at Salesian College in Bootle and Damian at West Park (now De La Salle), St Helens. They were founding members of the Heads of RE Association of the Liverpool Archdiocese and served on the Diocesan Vocations team under Fr Vincent. They were also active participators in the Loughborough Summer Schools where Damian showed himself to be a deep thinker, a superb liturgist and practitioner in catechesis for young people and a fine trainer of others. Jim remembers that on one of the sessions the housekeeper rushed in to tell everyone to watch the television. It was the broadcast which told about Bloody Sunday. When it was over everyone left in total and stunned silence. That evening at the liturgy Damian, responsible for organising the Penitential Rite, incorporated a sign of peace which embraced the events of Bloody Sunday. He had the sensitivity and the skill to bring the significance of the sins of the world into liturgy and prayer. During the same conference his group was assigned the Offertory Procession, and they decided to choreograph the procession through movement and dance. Two aisles, two groups: one represented the bread being kneaded and baked, the other the wine, grapes picked, crushed, turned into a cordial. Each process was interpreted with beauty, and each ended with the raising of hands and the reciting of the words "The work of human hands". At the time these offertory prayers were quite new and the dramatisation of the words was a powerful liturgical experience.

Damian had also gone on to Kintbury where he had been a pioneer in retreat work for young people, into in-service training for staff and catechists, developing music, writings and approaches to liturgy that were inclusive and recognised the skills that existed already in the parish. Then he went on to his Doctorate, the latter being specifically on adult catechesis since Vatican II, a focus that brought in so much of the Catholic community that was not school based.

It was at this point that the National Project team were looking for someone who could be a bridge between school, parish and family, young person and adult, the academic and the experiential. They were looking for a known and experienced communicator, one who encouraged partnership and inclusiveness. He had experience of Justice and Peace issues, having been part of a CAFOD fact finding mission to Central America. His reputation was worldwide. His book, *Growing into Faith*, written with Gerard Rummery, was already published and used vocabulary that had become part of the aims and objectives of the National Project. Was it any surprise that when the Committee met, the person top of their list was Damian?

So, in 1988 Damian joined an amazing group of people: he was delighted to be involved, passionately keen to contribute, eager to be of assistance nationally. Initially he was part-time because he was still working on his PhD; it was frustrating for Jim. His gifts were soon put to good use for consultation, and with Jim he visited hundreds of parishes and schools and met with thousands of teachers, catechists galore, youth groups, and heads, the very people who were dedicated to the faith in many different contexts, some at the cutting edge, some struggling perhaps, others eager to be involved. Damian was especially involved with the adult groups and he had the ability to help them turn their discussions into reality, to enable active participation by the reluctant or those who did not see themselves having relevant gifts. He always prepared his sessions meticulously and one part flowed naturally into another, each developing and deepening what went before. He was responsible for an in-service day for teachers from Lancashire Catholic schools which was held at Alston Hall in Longridge, the date May 2nd 1991. Whatever he did involved prayer, reflection, action, commitment, celebration. The process itself was evangelising, deepening, catechising. He always asked questions, gave time for personal reflection, invited response and commitment. He loved ecological metaphors, for they dealt with matters of life and death; he invited discussion, he used humour, stories, music. He shared Church documents most people had never heard of; on this occasion he quoted from the Declaration on Christian Education from Vatican II, a text published in 1965, and vitally relevant to the life and work of the Lancashire teachers.

"No less than other schools does the Catholic school pursue cultural goals and the natural development of youth. But it has several distinctive purposes. It aims to create for the school community an atmosphere enlivened by the Gospel spirit of freedom and charity. It aims to help adolescents in such a way that the development of their own personality will be matched by the growth of that new creation which they became at baptism. It strives to relate all human culture eventually to the news of salvation, so that the light of faith will illumine the knowledge which the students gain of the world, of life, and of humankind."

No wonder he used Deep Purple in Australia or that he invited the teachers to reflect on the reality before them. He would offer a selection of statistics and get them to tease out their implications in the classroom. In 1991 8 or 9 out of 10 people get married. 3 out of 5 new marriages will survive. 2 out of 5 will end in divorce. The UK has the highest divorce rate in Europe. Every year 150,000 children have parents who divorce. 52,000 of these children will be under 5. In the next ten years 3 million people will get divorced and some $1^1/2$ million children under 16 would be affected by it. If that was 1991, what about today? This is a reality facing each teacher, catechist, parish worker, parent... So he would ask: What do you do that promotes health and is life giving? What do you do that is life-threatening? The implications of the answers raise levels of awareness, so that staff can work collaboratively to ensure the life and health of the school (and by implication of family, parish and local community). He invited them to consider three responses: How could they promote three experiences of faith: head faith, heart faith, hands faith? It involved the whole person, the individual and the community. He was experiential, inclusive, active, responsive, willing to share, inviting others to discover their gifts and offer them in celebration and joy.

When it came to youngsters, he employed similar processes, making the material appropriate to their age and experience. He always met people where they were, he did not make assumptions or presume to impose on them. He made young people think. If they were primary school children he would invite them to reflect on *John Brown, Rose and the Midnight Cat*; with teenagers he would break the word, especially John's Gospel and the story of the Man born Blind. He was sparked off by writers and presenters like Maurice Lynch! Year after year Damian and Ann White would exchange exciting children's books they had found: "unless you become like little children..." What he disliked was "unpacked" doctrine or instruction that presumed knowledge and practise. As Jesus did in the parables, he used methods which challenged, which questioned, which demanded choice.

This was an immensely creative time for the National Project Team and Damian was delighted to be part of it, working with such well known experts as Vicky Cosstick, Declan Lang and John O'Shea on the resources for parishes. It was great to "be Church" now, bearing in mind the gifted group of people involved, and the rich contribution they made to resources for the Church. A simple list of people and their publications is breathtaking, for here is a gifted cross section of the Church community:

Our Faith Story, A.P. Purnell 1985.
Guidelines, Jim Gallagher, 1986.
All Is Gift, Lynn Walker, 1987.
Sharing the Gift, Paddy Rylands, 1989
Welcome, Jenny Pate, 1989
Our Schools and Our Faith, Jim Gallagher, 1988.
RE: The Primary Years, Danny Sullivan with Jim Gallagher, 1990.

Weaving the Web, Richard Lohan and Mary McClure, 1988.
Just Seniors, Judith Russi, 1990.
Easter Plus, Jenny Pate, 1991
To Be A People of Hope, A.P. Purnell, 1987.
Walking the Road, Dympna Magee, 1990.
From Barriers to Community, Mary Grey and Richard Zipfel, 1991.
Here I Am, Anne Byrne and Chris Malone,1992.
The Parish Project, Vicky Cosstick, Declan Lang, John O'Shea
    and Damian Lundy.
Family Plus, Jenny Pate.
Where two or three are Gathered, Mary McKeone and Damian Lundy.

The topics covered were wide ranging: insights into the National Project; Faith journey; Guidelines for parish catechists working with children; preparing to celebrate sacraments with families in the parish; celebrations with young children for the Church's year; school evaluation and ethos; Primary School RE; a modular programme for RE; resources on Justice and Peace issues; family celebrations; family activities from Lent to Pentecost; family activities for the Church's year; adult Education, a Christian perspective; Reflections on the Gospel story; the challenge of the Gospel for a divided society; resources for parishes to enable them to set out and work at priorities; a post-Confirmation programme.

What a disappointment that Jim had to acknowledge at the beginning of his article that the very existence of the National Project of Catechesis and Religious Education may come as news to some readers: news not only that the Project is nearly ten years old, but news that there is such a thing as the National Project. These were golden days! What a gathering of characters, vocations, expertise, gifts, humanity, depth, spirituality, scholarship. These were people who invited all to become more mature and committed in faith. In a way, the National Project was like Mark's parable of the seed growing secretly: gradually day and night, unknown to many, it came to fruition. So much of what they did and how they did it looked to this model. When it comes to evangelisation and catechesis it's hard to beat Jesus!

That the experience was vital and energising was demonstrated by Jim, Bernadette and Anne when they recalled these days. They went to the heart of the matter and relived the vision, the joy, the excitement, the frustrations, the great sense of working as a team.

> Damian promoted it by living it, not just by telling it; he'd done it; he knew it was the right thing to do; he knew this was what the Church should be and was asking us to be. He felt so deeply about it; his way of working came out of a very deep conviction and theology of Church and lay people.

The team was convinced that they were the traditionalists in the Church, for their work and its development came from the heart of Church documents. Damian himself, having reflected on the whole experience of working on the project, remarked that St Augustine in *De catechizandis rudibus* had it easy in comparison with the Church today! Damian had the mind and the heart for the project but was frequently frustrated by unwieldy structures, the divisive opposition, the ignorance of what the Church actually taught, and the pernickety approach to words. He used to get very angry with people who thought he was clever enough to be a priest. He was very proud to be a *lay* religious, and this gave him insight into, and great respect for, the richness of the whole Church community, all of whose members are called to holiness but by different ways of life. This was why the process involved widespread consultation, a slow, frustrating, and messy but necessary business, one which drew in the wisdom and Spirit in the whole community and which was by nature and by choice inclusive.

Serious it was, but there were plenty of moments of joy and fun. Laughter was integral to living the process. When Jim and Damian arrived they had no offices or desks. They were lodged in a corridor. However, at the end of the corridor was a french window which gave onto a balcony overlooking Cromwell Road and the Natural History Museum. Here, after work on warm Summer evenings, Jim, Damian, Bernadette, Anne and others would sit, sipping the occasional beverage, telling stories, laughing and making community. Jim and Damian were such contrasting characters. By his own admission, Jim lives on his nerves, in a rush, keen to get on; Damian (making good use of his conviction that physical rushing around is not good for the health) was more measured, admiring, attentive to pictures on walls, views from windows. It meant that stories were told, music was listened to, little *trattoria* patronised. It was great to be Church now!

Anne remembers occasions when she and Damian worked together, testing, trying, creating. One significant time was a conference for CATSC in the Cherwell Centre, Oxford, when the theme was Lent for Primary School children. The general feeling was that they should begin with Ash Wednesday. Not so! Anne intervened. We must begin with Shrove Tuesday – Carnival, celebration, in a way preparing to say goodbye to things. Everything became experiential: groups were encouraged to be creative in presenting the themes to primary children, and off they went. Anne vividly remembers one group which created a helter-skelter big dipper that showed life's ups and downs; another became a train and journeyed accordingly. Damian was immersed in it, full of laughter and fun. He was indeed childlike, in touch with a key characteristic of the Kingdom.

Another was a day for the Primary Heads Conference in Shrewsbury Diocese when his theme was the Man Born Blind. He turned his presentation into a dialogue and engaged the Heads naturally, thoughtfully and creatively. His ability to enable others led to an amazing self-effacement. John the Baptist's "He must become more and more, I less and less" (Jn 3:30) was so natural to Damian; if others came into their own it led to delight and celebration. He found it harder to cope with those who, also in John, preferred the dark and blindness. These days, the pattern of Genesis is renewed: "There came a pharaoh who knew not Joseph." It is normal to come across things happening, diagrams, prayers, reflections, little dramas, schemes of questions that are common currency, the users not knowing the origin. Often they are in Damian. Anne mentioned a young catechist who was excited about a diagram of 4 squares and a diamond that enabled personal reflection. Damian's.

They all remember the occasions they met during August 1991 in a small room in Anne's flat in Dulwich to draw up a diagrammatic overview of the *Here I Am*. The poster was to help parents, teachers and parish priests to see on a single sheet the whole process over a three year period. It showed that not everything needed to be done in the first year, either the subject matter or the different depths that were possible in the development of the students. The language was adapted to the age of the participants, and the overview showed how Church vocabulary was introduced gradually in parallel with the knowledge and experience offered by the programme and its resources.

On one occasion Jim was returning late from a consultation and decided to call in to the offices in Cromwell Road to collect his post. As he arrived he found someone trying to open the door; when he saw Jim he fled. Jim found he could not open the door with his key (the lock was known to be temperamental). He suddenly heard bells ringing, and within minutes three fire engines arrived at the door. Just at that point, Damian emerged from the entrance of the hotel next to the offices and spent a long time trying to convince the fire officer that there was not a fire. Damian had been working late and the last person to leave (thinking the building was empty) had deadlocked the door. Damian could not get out. He tried everything and eventually telephoned his community house in Victoria Road and asked for help. The only one in at the time was Vittorio, a Brother from Lebanon, who was convalescing after a bomb attack on his school. Vittorio came round and Damian threw his key out of the window. Vittorio tried the lock, couldn't open it, felt like a thief, came face to face with Jim and fled! Damian, not wishing to spend the night in the building, had decided to use the fire exit at the top of the building. It led directly to the hotel next door. Unfortunately, the door was alarmed and as soon as he opened it all hell broke loose. When the engines arrived, Jim scarpered! After all, there wasn't a fire. The fire officer went into the building via the hotel and was taken aback by what he saw. "We shall be back," was his terse comment. Return he did, made a thorough inspection, demanded significant improvements and the works ran up a bill of over £20,000.

In a way it was Damian who helped to bring the whole thing together (the project, not the fire improvements) and Anne remembers going to Oxford to sit with him, discussing and arranging while he was on his haemodialysis machine in Churchill Hospital. It was bad enough liaising with the many different authors, but the consultation involved thousands! Then it all had to be referred "above" and sometimes "above" asked for changes of things that had already been argued over and refined. The team acknowledge their debt to Vincent Nichols who as General Secretary gave final approval, for he kept them going, he worked with them, was a kind of signpost for them. Infinitely patient he supported and encouraged; he made them feel that their work was part of a significant contribution to the life of the Church.

It had not been a painless process, and in an eloquent article in *The Tablet*, 22nd February 1992, Damian and Jim offer important insights into *Weaving the Web*.

> Many teachers bear witness that pupils in the first three years of secondary school find the *Weaving the Web* programme attractive and engaging. But its value has recently been the subject of fierce debate. Br Damian Lundy and Fr Jim Gallagher explain just what the programme is designed to do.
>
> In recent months there has been considerable controversy over the religious education programme *Weaving the Web*, both in the Catholic and national press. We believe that *Weaving the Web* is a major contribution to the renewal and development of religious education in Catholic schools for pupils between the ages of 11 and 14 (Key Stage 3) and that it represents probably the most important contribution that the Catholic Church in England and Wales has offered to religious education in schools which are not Catholic. It was, for example, highly recommended in the *Times Educational Supplement*. In the

Decade of Evangelisation, that is something of which we can be proud.

Some, however, see this as one of the main weaknesses of the programme. If it is used in schools which are not Catholic, they argue, it cannot be Catholic enough. While we defend the programme, we acknowledge that it has its limitations and that it is not always used wisely. We are at present co-ordinating the work of diocesan advisers and others who are studying ways in which the programme may be improved and ways in which teachers may be helped to use it more effectively.

Critics of *Weaving the Web* have disparaged even the programme's title. Its authors, Richard Lohan and Mary McClure SND, contend that RE, "like the spider's web that catches everything that comes its way... has to do with all aspects of life and religion". Critics often quote Pope John Paul II's apostolic exhortation *Catechesi Tradendae* (1979) when pointing out what they perceive to be the limitations of the *Web*. Yet the web metaphor is used in that very papal text: "Revelation tells of the radical change of man and the universe, of all that makes up the web of human life under the influence of the Good News of Jesus Christ."

Granted the validity of the web metaphor to describe human life, what of the Pope's reference to revelation and the Good News of Jesus Christ? These are claimed by some to be absent from *Weaving the Web*. We detect five main criticisms of the books: 1. The programme is said to have got its priorities wrong: incomplete and superficial, it omits several key truths of Catholic doctrine; 2. Too much emphasis is placed on encouraging young people to explore their own experiences: too many of its learning intentions are experimental; 3. There is excessive study of non-Christian religions: this could lead to syncretism, a special danger in view of the way the programme underplays Christianity and the Catholic tradition; 4. The authors give too much attention (so argues Piers Paul Read in his pamphlet *Quo Vadis*) to "some of the enthusiasms of the alternative magisterium" such as liberation theology and feminism; 5. The programme justifies its content by describing itself as a programme of religious education and by distinguishing this from catechesis (education in faith) although Catholic schools exist to teach and promote the Catholic faith.

Let us reflect briefly on at least some aspects of these criticisms. But, first, we could ask who is expressing them five years after publication of the programme (many critics still refer to it as "new"). RE teachers are more likely than some parents and clergy to defend *Weaving the Web*. Is this because RE teachers are more likely to be liberal Catholics, or is it because they are more in touch with the practical difficulties of teaching RE in Britain today to young people from a variety of religious experiences and background (even among those who profess to be Catholic)?

Though distinctions need to be made between critics of *Weaving the Web*, most who have taken part in the recent controversy in the press would be happy to see themselves described as conservative Catholics. They are very conscious of the threats facing religious belief in modern society; they are anxious about misrepresentations of Vatican II by which, they say, liberals justify their theological errors (as the first part of Read's pamphlet makes clear); they are unhappy about some policies of the Bishops' Conference of England and Wales and of the approach taken by some individual bishops.

How valid are the criticisms? By its own admission, *Weaving the Web* is incomplete if judged as a summary or overview of the full range of Catholic doctrine. Religious education spans the nursery years to the final year of sixth form (4–18); *Weaving the Web* covers only three of these years (11–14) and even then does not claim to be a complete scheme of work to be used lesson by lesson: "This programme does not set out to provide a script for teachers nor a self-contained sequenced learning programme for the pupil to complete in isolation. There is a basic framework..., a selection of learning intentions to be selected from or augmented, ...tasks and extension activities as a platform for building on" (to quote from the *Weaving the Web* teachers' book). In Catholic schools, of course, time will be given to the liturgical seasons, particular feasts and other aspects of Catholic life.

Many seem to misunderstand the tool that is being offered and a number of teachers misuse it, especially if they are not qualified in RE This raises important and relevant questions about the recruitment and training of RE teachers, the real position of RE in the overall curriculum planning (as opposed to the fine phrases that may appear in a mission statement or school prospectus), the management of RE departments, the time available for department meetings to introduce a new programme and to draw up and evaluate a scheme of work suited to the needs of the pupils in each school.

It is important to look at the ways *Weaving the Web* is being used in some schools. There is no perfect text which will overcome all the deficiencies in some schools and individual teachers. *Weaving the Web* offers a framework which provides for continuity, cohesion and progression in RE in Key Stage 3. Many heads of RE find it a welcome and useful aid in drawing up and shaping their own scheme of work. The question has to asked, "What were schools using before?" One head of RE who drew attention to some limitations of the programme nevertheless expressed his gratitude for a helpful framework. Before the *Web* he and his department had to construct their own programme entirely from scratch. The *Web* also provided a sound educational basis for RE which was much appreciated by teachers and pupils.

In Britain today many Catholic religious educators of teenagers see their main challenge as how to motivate young people to appreciate the value and relevance of Christian faith in a secularised and pluralistic world. The Vatican document *The Religious Dimension of Education in a Catholic School* (1988) remarks that "For many young people, a critical look at the world they are living in leads to crucial questions on the religious plane". While acknowledging that "large numbers of them sincerely want to know how to deepen their faith and live a meaningful life", it also recognises that, influenced by what they see and hear, "perhaps some have become indifferent or insensitive". It goes on to say that "doubt and indifference are common phenomena, and the reasons for this are readily understandable".

Pupils of this mix are in our Catholic schools. The pupils' books of *Weaving the Web* set over twenty tasks or activities in each of the six modules which involve the pupils actively in exploration and discussion of, and reflection on, some of these crucial questions and how Christian beliefs and practices (and those of some other faith traditions) relate to them.

It may be useful to recall here the theological distinction between *fides quae* and *fides qua*: between the faith of the

Church on the one hand and, on the other, the journey of faith by which a person come to make that faith his or her own. This varies from person to person and while such a journey can be encouraged and made possible, it can never be demanded or forced. It is for this reason that in *Weaving the Web* sentences are likely to begin "Christians believe...", "Catholics profess..." The aim is not to stand back in a clinically neutral stance (such a stance is never possible), nor to encourage syncretism, but to acknowledge that all pupils cannot be assumed to be believers. Whatever their own position may be, however, pupils are led to a knowledge and understanding of such beliefs and practices. They are also encouraged to examine their own religious attitude and to respect that of others.

The religious lesson will have different results for different pupils; for all it will be religious education, for some evangelisation and for others catechesis. It is implied by critics in a frequently quoted passage from *Guidelines and Our Schools and Our Faith* that Fr Jim Gallagher, one of the co-ordinators of the National Project, holds that RE lessons are in no way connected with the development or nurture of faith. Such is a misunderstanding, as one paragraph in *Guidelines* seeks to make clear. Entitled "Distinct but Overlapping", it says: "While religious education does not necessarily presume Christian faith, it may well lead to the deepening of faith in some. . . All should be better informed and have a more sensitive understanding of the Christian way of life, even if they cannot commit themselves to it." However inadequate the wording might be, it is an attempt to work out in practice what is stated about the distinct yet complementary nature of catechesis and RE in part four of the Vatican document already referred to, *The Religious Dimension of Education in a Catholic School*. Other texts of the National Project discuss the role of the school in the work of catechesis and the Christian vision which should permeate all aspects of school life. It is within such a context that *Weaving the Web* is offered as a framework for RE lessons.

In our view there is in the programme considerably more Catholic and Christian features than many critics imply. There is certainly a strong experiential approach because, particularly in the teenage years, "experience serves in the examination and acceptance of the truths which are contained in the deposit of revelation", as the *General Catechetical Directory* puts it. It should be remembered that teachers are expected to select from the tasks which deal with the experiences of the pupils, not to do them all. Some can be done in conjunction with other departments in a cross-curricular approach. Some schools succeed extremely well in this. If teachers simply follow all tasks slavishly, it is more a matter for in-service instruction than a cry for a text for the weak, unimaginative teacher. Work has already started on preparing practical resources for such in-service training.

Let us take the module on community. At level one (the first year of secondary school) pupils are stimulated to be aware of and describe the communities to which they belong. An exploration of Christianity in the local community is included: this leads to a set of tasks on baptism as initiation into the Church. In two tasks pupils are invited to examine the contrasting lifestyles of young people in Peru. Four tasks explore aspects of Hinduism more relevant to people of their own age, in particular a Hindu naming ceremony.

At level two, tasks concentrate on the different roles and responsibilities of people in community. This includes roles and ministries in parishes and dioceses. Five tasks use the teaching of Jesus and Paul to examine responsibilities in the Christian community. The theme of Jesus as the servant of others is explored in two tasks. The responsibilities within their community of Jewish teenagers is looked at (two tasks). One task considers a family in the Third World.

The analysis of community deepens at level three, which focuses on the way communities experience and deal with conflict. At this age, conflict in family and within oneself is a real and deep experience. Several tasks invite the pupils to explore such conflicts. Five tasks explore Christian ideas about healing and reconciliation, including the sacrament of reconciliation. One task looks at the Muslim community and another touches on the Christian ecumenical movement.

Such an overview of one module over the three years should serve to show the developmental and experiential approach of the programme and the key aspects of the Christian tradition which are studied within this one module out of the six. It should also show that the study of other faiths is hardly excessive. In each of the three years a relevant feature of another religion is considered: Hinduism/Buddhism (1st year), Judaism

(2nd year), Muslim (3rd year). In our pluralist society this seems educationally sound and theologically in line with Vatican II. It is also in response to the request of the English and Welsh bishops at their Low Week meeting of 1982 that any new programme be suited "to the multi-cultural and multi-faith background of our people". The aim is not to endorse or encourage relativism but rather "to ensure tolerance, respect and understanding between all cultures and traditions represented not only in the school or its immediate environment, but in the country as a whole" (*Evaluating the Distinctive Nature of a Catholic School*).

Much of this may seem far removed from the kind of RE lessons familiar to an older generation. One head of RE, praising the easy continuity between the experiential and more specifically theological material, explained to us how his third year secondary pupils were led, through an examination of conflict within themselves, to ask for a class celebration of the sacrament of reconciliation. This helped to convince him of the value of using experience as a starting point with teenagers rather than using articles of Catholic teaching which would be foreign to many of them. The frame of reference is experiential, so adult concepts are approached in a way which makes them more accessible to young people in 1992.

Teachers are expected to select from and augment tasks and materials to meet needs and abilities of the pupils as well as the constraints of the timetable (normally about three periods of 40 minutes a week). Each module is designed as a framework for a half a term's work. This means that in the course of each of the first three years of secondary school pupils will explore aspects of Church (community), Scripture (story), Jesus, Mary, saints (people), worship, prayer (communication), sacraments (celebration), the Christian way of life (values). If some modules only are used, key aspects of the Christian tradition will be neglected. This happens in schools which have not purchased all six pupils' books or where no selection of tasks is made. This is to misuse *Weaving the Web*.

Before recent critics of the *Web* became vociferous, as co-ordinators of the National Project we had already set up a working party to evaluate the use of the programme in Catholic schools. It is clear that some more practical aids are needed to enable RE departments to draw up a scheme of work and to enable teachers to plan and pace their lessons by setting out criteria for the selection of tasks and for augmenting the resources provided in *Weaving the Web*. Much of this falls within the responsibility of diocesan advisers.

The recent controversy over *Weaving the Web* has been useful in so far as it has highlighted various aspects of a complex issue. It has also been far from helpful as it was often conducted with anger and bitterness which, on occasions, showed little respect for persons and their integrity. The whole thrust of the National Project seeks to encourage the necessary partnership which should exist between all involved in educating the young to and in faith: home, parish, school and the young themselves. It is important to recognise that for many it is a matter of education to faith not in faith.

It is a pity that some seem too ready to point the finger in condemnation rather than to join hands in the common task which is neither simple nor easy. Reading the Gospels shows that it was not simple or easy for Jesus. Cardinal Martini has a homily in his book *Ministers of the Gospel* entitled "Jesus the failed evangelist". The title and the text are worthy of our reflection and meditation in the context of educating to and in faith especially in the Decade of Evangelisation.

Jim sees this as a kind of "Pro vita sua" for Damian. It shows in miniature his vision of and for the Church: inclusive, experiential, deep, spiritual, Spirit-filled, Gospel-based, in which no one is ontologically different from anyone else.

They and others have many "blurred happy memories", a remembering of what seemed like golden days, wondering where the great catechists and evangelisers are today.

While Damian was involved in the National Project he continued to make contacts nationwide, and to be involved in numerous offshoots of the programme. Sr Maeve McDevitt gives her insights into the establishment of the Key Catechists programme:

> In 1989 I approached Br Damian, he was National Adviser for RE, and asked if he could help get a National Centre for the formation of Key Catechists off the ground. Mount Oliver, Dundalk, was about to close and there was not anywhere in the

British Isles for the formation of professional or key people who in turn could train those in the parishes for the work of catechesis. Catechesis at parish level was, and still is, a growing ministry in the Church. We approached the Conference of Religious for help. At first two members were sent to speak to us.

They asked us to write a paper stating what we required. We were then asked to speak to the executive. As a result of this further meeting the COR gave a grant of £5,000 to research the need at national level. Sr Joan Yates chaired a working party and many members from the different dioceses were part of it. A questionnaire was sent to each diocese and to each seminary and college of education to ensure that we were not duplicating work already being done. We found that dioceses were more than willing to back the initiative and nowhere did we find that specific formation for catechists was being carried out. We sent a report of our findings to the Bishops' Conference of England and Wales who asked that a further questionnaire be sent to the seminaries and appointed Fr Kevin McGinnell, Sr Pat Murphy and Sr Ellen, formerly of Nottingham Diocese, to work with three of us from the old working party. We had a brief to look at funding, the seminaries and the likely location of such an institution.

We finished our task and sent the results to the Bishops' Conference. We awaited a reply, but none came. In the meantime Damian had visited Australia and did some research as to how they trained their catechists. I visited Canada and the United States and brought back many programmes. Eventually it was the programme for the formation of Permanent Deacons and Lay Ministers in the Indian reserves of Rapid City Diocese, *Builders of the New Earth*, that we adapted for our needs. It was important to us to integrate Spirituality, Theology and the process of Catechesis in the formation programme. When we got tired of waiting for a response from the Bishops' Conference I suggested that I start a pilot group and that is how the Newman Course for the Formation of Key Catechists began. It was Damian who named it as it was then the centenary of the death of Cardinal Newman.

Archbishop Vincent Nichols, who was then newly appointed as Bishop in North London, "canonically missioned" the first group of successful Key Catechists. Two years later

Northampton Diocese adopted the programme and last year East Anglia joined.

Without Damian's help and encouragement it would never have started. We now have housed in a special room in Hendon a reference library where many of Damian's books on theology, scripture, sacraments and catechesis are. They were generously donated by Brother Joseph Hendron, Damian's Provincial, as a tribute to Damian after his death. So his memory and spirit live on and we remember him with deep gratitude.

Damian was invited to the inauguration of the new Catechetical Centre in Milton Keynes under the directorship of Fr Kevin McGinnell. The Centre has a wonderful address: Our Lady of Lourdes, Lloyds, Coffee Hall, Milton Keynes! CATSC has an annual conference and the first item on its agenda is the Damian Lundy Memorial Lecture.

Damian became involved in a book to promote an understanding of the Second Vatican Council, to make it accessible to parishes and Sixth formers. The book was the joint work of Louisa Pool SSL, Christopher Jamison OSB and Damian Lundy FSC. Louisa, who had been involved in the parish project which led to the publication, gives us the background and history of it all.

Fr Guy Sawyer, the Parish Priest of The Sacred Heart of Jesus and St John the Evangelist, Bushey, gave great support to the Director of Adult Education, Peter Keenan, who put on a series of Lenten courses over a number of years, and these were attended by some forty people. The excellent response encouraged them to develop the idea and offer further study and action. In 1991–1992, Peter Keenan and Louisa suggested that the group might very usefully look at the documents of Second Vatican Council since it was this event that had changed the shape of the Church in the 20th century. The plan looked something like this: small groups would work on individual documents; the main documents would be summarised and then the whole would be shared with the large group which in turn would find ways of sharing the results with the Parish as a whole.

It was amazing! The involvement was really good, discussions were marvellously thorough as well as heated at times. Getting to grips with the work of the Council was a real education, since it brought up so many issues of past teaching and history. Small groups tackled the summarising of documents, and great work was done. Everybody developed a great respect for the Council. Every phase was shared with the parish at large, in an ongoing series of inputs to the Sunday Liturgy by members of the group. On completion of these phases of the project it was suggested that other parishes might benefit.

The National Project was contacted, with a view to extending the work to a wider stage; this was really ambitious. The scale of the work was reviewed and the idea broached of a comprehensive look at the documents as a whole which would benefit local churches and students. Clearly someone needed to work on this more systematically and Louisa was asked and agreed to take on the writing tasks, and do the first draft of summaries of the documents.

In June 1992, Louisa had her first meetings with Damian. Initially, some of the committee did not look too enthusiastically at the proposed work but perseverance and solid faith kept the small group going. When Damian's work on the National Project was complete he joined Louisa on the work, though it also coincided with a dramatic decline in his health. Christopher was introduced by Damian since the historical origins of the Council were his special interest and the three continued the work. After numerous sessions at Worth and in Kensington, and then in Oxford, the structure was decided and each one took specific parts of the text to develop. The final text was to reflect its origins in the parish and be "user-friendly", readable and clear, with ordinary readers and students in mind. Anne White, representing the National Project, came in on matters of presentation, and did a wonderful job.

The launch was a great occasion and Anne had arranged for Vaughan House to be available; Archbishop Worlock led the occasion, supported by Bishop Konstant. It was the culmination of an initiative started in Bushey and which now influences catechists, parish groups, seminarians, and students throughout the English speaking world.

Another mustard seed becomes a tree!

10 | Damian's Poems Songs and Hymns

In this chapter are gathered some of Damian's unpublished poems, songs and hymns, amusing and serious. For some Damian left particular notes, for others, a short note has been added because there is something particular about the song or poem which deserves to be noted.

HALIFAX

I love your plain dark bridges, streets, old lighted shops,
With bells and wooden blinds, and heavy odours: smells
And shelves of blankets; market floors; cooked meats on
    marble slabs.
In railway carriages I smell them. I love them and you.

One evening on your railway line: a rattle, whistle, whoop
Of joy! and factory windows cast warm glows
Into the dusty brown compartments; outside rows
And rows of doors, brown brickstone, aching walls,

And friendly and familiar; and kitchen windows
Spin into coloured points and fade before old parish-halls,
Churches and crooked railings, lost
Into your yellow light. They lurk behind, crouch low, are
    happy. Spires stoop

To smoking chimneys, chimneys massive and black, strong,
    sheltered back
And panting beneath the great high hills, your moors and
    hills, your hills that brood
Over your tower, town, lights, all spread safe and far below
    and fine.

And, all around, your rooftops greet grey night, and in the
    smoke are gay
And clatter and sing as signals flash, and whistles and
    engines whine.
Then choking smoke, steamed windows, and sad sooted
    tunnel-walls black you out and away.

*I wrote this poem about Halifax a short time ago. Perhaps you
would like to read it? One day I'll write one about Sowerby
Bridge too. Michael.*

Damian's social occasions often ended with a good story,
humour, fun and a creative writing time. The first few pages in
this chapter give access to a range of these. So our visiting of
Damian ends as many remember him, with a menu of laughter
and smiles, of coping with pain and disappointment, with insights,
and with some dots... He was comfortable with the open-ended
nature of life, since people, experiences and questions were for
him God's encouragement to other deeper searchings. It is good
to give him the last words.

Story I

A bullfrog called Julius Caesar
Made eyes at a toad called Teresa.
"Look here!" said a drake
To the bullfrog: "You rake!
I have told you before not to tease her."

Story II

The toad said: "I love him, you purit –
an! Drake said: "Well, I'll not endure it!
Corrupting the neighbours…
Disgusting, bejabbers!
I'll stop you - I'll send for the curate!"

Story III

A clerical newt, Ebenezer,
Preached fire and brimstone: "I'll freeze her
With fright – that'll stop her,
Or she'll 'come a cropper'!
He said, of loose-living Teresa.

Story IV + V

The toadess would not be converted.
She said: "Sir, why! I've only flirted
A little! That's nothin'!"
"When you're in your coffin,"
The newt said, "THEN you'll be averted!

"Too late, ma'm - too late! You'll be caught up
With, then! You will die, ma'm, distraught. Up
We'll go to our glory
But YOU…" (End of story:

A crocodile swallowed the lot up!)

OTHERS

In the winter the river froze down in
Its bottomest depths, almost drownin'
With cold a poor creature
Or two. "That'll teach yer!"
The ice whispered, nastily frowning.

"Spring has come! Banish Care – let's discard her!"
Said Sir Drake to his Duck. Their armada
Sailed, not knowing that
Up was creeping a Rat!
Mother Nature had opened her larder.

A butterfly housewife went shoppin'.
Alas! her antillae caught up in
A whiff of stray cloud;
But her screams were so loud,
They dissolved it – and rain drops came droppin'!

When the floods came, the river was belching
As hippos do when they are rel'shing
Food! Lord Pike blew his nose.
Lady Reed wet her toes,
And things in the mud started squelching.

Sir Tad Pole protected the river –
Or part of it! He had a quiver
Of arrows to fire at
Marauder or pirate
Or brigand! And he made them shiver

With fright, if ever they came near:
His countenance filled them with fear.
And when they had fled
And the river was dead
Calm, he treated himself to a beer!

The river flowed over a star, lick
ing shades phosphorescent. Lights frolic
ing glimmered. The day
Breathed hard. "Get away!"
Said the water: "You've been eating garlic!"

A willow tree couldn't stop weeping.
It worried him, stopped him from sleeping:
So he went to a clinic
For treatment. A cynic –
al French nurse said: "Ô! you arre drreeping!"

There once was a bullrush called Gruddle,
Who grew in a permanent puddle.
And then came a drought
When the water ran out:
Said Gruddle: "Gosh! I'm in a muddle."

TO GOD THE FATHER
(First Sunday in Lent – Psalm 50)

O Lord, you search me and you know me,
in all the holes of my heart You hide to reproach me.
The Rabbit, alone on his grassland,
catches the scarcely audible first sound of a human footfall,
and He runs: I run when I hear you,
flee to my hole for I fear You, fear
your ways, so scamper to darkness, bristle and be still;
stiff ears held high, eyes rounded white and wide
in the heavy blackness. O, then, O, feel warm firm fingers,
    a father's hand
being gentle and strong, a Father's Hand, and the drift of breath
being warm and following through, and the tightening
    Father Hand,
and the face and eyes of God; the nearing light… then,
    the gentle tug
is done, and between hand and heart I nestle, and no band
    to shut me there.
Know me, and hold me, God, and never loosen Hand and Hug.

TO GOD THE SON
(A sonnet for Lent)

Christ for man maimed,
the coppergilded Fish did never green
because some man spilt acid in the seas;
nor did the Sunlight curdle, thicken, freeze,
before man's made white light, fired in man's bulb;
Neither did flashing Dragonfly in air pressed, prismed lie
and all its hues congealed, split, stripped; nor olive trees,
choked by self gendered oil, grow black and die.
But You, the Master-hand, -mind, -heart, and -all,
God by nature and name, became man's slave: poor
Child of poor mother, cowcribbed; poor broken Man
bared, bruised, greened, prismed, choked to death
Child on mother's lap, no nature: own Reverse, divinely wild
    and willed
Godact – Christ's ransom of Christ's choosing –
Christ, o Christ, o kind, so kind.

TO CLIVE
(Mark 10:38)

"All we are called to do is love."
For one afraid to live alone
That's easy talk! The language failed
To probe its way through skin and bone
Into your heart. You laughed aloud.
The echoes still resound in me,
Shaping the landscape of a dream:
Your dark eyes smile defiantly.

I've searched for gestures. How to prove
I'm chosen to bear witness to
Compulsive metaphors: to save
Drowning children who scream to know
If they are loved? That "if" appals

Me, when I hesitate to dive
Into dark swirling water below,
To snatch from death, restore to life.

I fear the dazzling waterfall's
Attendant dangers and delights,
Where all the wounded dreamers go.
I long for other ways to show
Concern for you. They're not enough!
Echoes resound, ambitions live:
All I am called to do is love,
To plunge, to rescue, to forgive –

And be forgiven, too, for I,
When stripped of shallow laughter, stand
Naked and scared, haunted by doubts
Not even you would understand.
We share the darkness. Oh, may all
The stones which block both hearts be rolled
Away, to reveal the love I knew
Mere words would not make flesh for you.

Rome
February 1979

The poems on pages 213–215 were published with accompanying comments in the Australian magazine *Word in Life*, May 1979.

Initiation Song

November 1987
(No music)

In the word of our God we find new hope,
To the praying of Christ we join our prayer,
By the Spirit of love our lives are healed,
In the house of God we come to share.

In the water of life we know God's power,
In the sign of the cross God's love is shown,
In the bread and wine Christ gives himself
To the ones he chose to be his own.

And the Easter flame is our sign of joy,
The good news of our God, our Easter song,
And the gift of faith, our call to share
Now the oil of Christ has made us strong.

All the people of God give thanks today
To the Father who saves, to Christ his Son,
To the Holy Spirit in whom we know
The restoring love which makes us one.

The Man

*To Terry McLaughlin, Hubert Richards, and all who belong to the
experience and share the knowledge.*

I know you
Out of the mirror you burst and stagger me,
you, man, with a too familiar face.
I know you.
You are the one who strides out of the crowd.
In your eyes I see myself,
caught in your flesh, your being.

You have known all, felt all,
knowledge of good and evil
salty and warm in tears, sticky in blood.
What knowledge! What compassion! Too hard
to bear! You sigh under that burden.
It weighs on your body and pulls you down from the crossbar.
Your blood is on my hand. It is warm.
You die in my arms.
Shocked and timid, guiltily I tiptoe to cover your naked corpse.
Bury it! Cover it! It grins in the dark.

We come together, the shocked and silent people
to entomb you in our memories and devotions,
embalm you in plaster
and nail you with jewels to gold.
We hoist you on to rood-screens, higher, higher.
You hang over altars, going brown with stain of incense-smoke.
Old sepia plaster-eyes!
You, man with a too familiar face!
I know you, sir,
but find you hard to place.

And now, suddenly,
you burst out of the plaster.
The tomb explodes – a living man appears.
And here am I.
And here I kneel, stretch out my hands to touch you,
and handle a glory in sweat, skin, in falling tears,
see you in sad old men and laughing children,
in human flesh, in a breathing mirror, a father bending over
    a child,
and I find a God, smiling.

Llandudno, 13th October 1973

To Rowena and Gwynn on Your Wedding Day

Affection moves my pen: its point
Scratches, the metre's out of joint.
I think of all those mused rhymes
We've shared together and all the times
We've known: like dead leaves in my mind –
Nostalgia's children! All unkind,
The winds of separation blow
Time's leaves into the bonfire's glow.

And yet the mood is blessed: today
Is full of dancing not dismay.
The October sky glows warm and rare
As wedding music fills the air
And the Future's door swings open to
Reveal the joys I'd wish for you,
Dear Friends, in praying God may be
Good to you and your family.

I pray that you'll construct a home
To welcome seasons as they come;
Then shall no winters barren be
For you, nor for your company;
And may the echoing rafters shake
With joyful noise that children make –
Jubilant laughter more than tears
(Though midnight cries assail your ears);

And may your children grow to be
All you desire and still be free
To be themselves – as you have been –
And may they see what you have seen
(I mean good things you would keep
For dreams, to see again in sleep);
May they your dearest interests share;
God keep them from the bitter care

Which can destroy a person's love;
May their imagination move
With that dexterity they'll see
Their mother to possess (for she
is rich in words and fleet of hand);
Their father's quiet steadiness stand
Them in good stead; so, they will be
Blessed with a fine security.

May summers fill your memory's store
With all the fruit you're longing for.
May darker seasons with their days
Of sacrifice and serious ways
Of fortitude and patience bear
Fruitful rewards you both will share,
And all the love you know still prove
The channel of more copious love.

As age advances by degrees
May comfort and domestic ease
Glow warm through your maturing years,
Burning anxieties and fears
Out of your life; while, all around,
New friends your table will surround.
What reaping! All the seeds you sow
Into a golden harvest grow.

Dear friends, your life together will
More than a single lifetime fill.
Entwined as one, by Heaven's grace,
You'll know God's kiss, his dear embrace,
And will a source of blessing be
Even to celibates like me,
Who celebrate your wedding-time
With inky flowers and formal rhyme.

With love! October 1975

AT ROBERT'S FUNERAL

Their eyes are swollen; the skin
hangs from them, brown and suddenly very
old and empty. I think of a favourite chair
with its arms rubbed dirty. They are dazed
with grief. Familiar times and gestures
break out of their minds, each one freeing the next;
or his old sayings, the well-worn family jokes
ache in their depths and make them want
to smile and then cry louder. Their loss
plunges me into their lives, and total strangers
are brothers, father, mother, me.
Death is a great womb
teeming with many children. Now am I
of his family, with these mourners one,
and the resemblance spreads upon my skin,
staining it very damp and suddenly very
swollen like theirs. Today, Robert,
buried in earth, you have become an old friend for many.
And I, who never knew you,
maybe never spoke to you,
mourn for my lost familiar child.

KERYGMA

(to Christ: a celebration)

God's great love and promise to men, his faithfulness, is
silent wonderwork of the Spirit breathing in Mary's womb
His living Word, forging the splendid flawless bond
of the Incarnation's union of God and Man in Christ.

Of whose veins, the blood was brewed by the Spirit of God
to be drunk by men; who is the Father's Son, Men's Brother:
The GodMan Christ, born to be broken, made to be maimed,
made man for the kiss of Judas who kissed agonised split

into the God-Man marriage. Scattered Christ's Blood will wed man
to God! the cry from the cross, his loneliness of pain and bitter
desolation; prismed light of Christ in heaven and hell

till, shining out and glorified, comes Hero God of Easter night,
my Brother! Christ, receive our joy from us united
to You, made one in Risen You, in Your new life and love fixed tight.

(1964: 25th March is Wednesday in Holy Week)

A SEQUENCE OF FOUR

"He with his body…"
W.B. Yeats: *The Four Ages of Man*

I: THE PLANTING

I bundled
a tree on a cold day, leaping
into the cold
planting a brown twig.

I
knelt down
out of the elements and
heaped on the earth's
mound scraping a burrow

deep
down and
poking. The force in the soil, the root
life pressed on a root
and the blowing wind

wind
which froze
hands and root together,
and pressed,
pulled into two again

then,
and I
with hands washed in the rain
hearing a wild owl hooting over
a twig dead in the rain

so hung down,
till a night animal
over the dead stalk
almost silently and not seeing

me,
crept past
and was never seen to move
until the tree
blossomed.

II For Teilhard in New York

Remember the tree at home, that pear tree
growing up in our garden, and the gay spring,
joli mai! the branches bursting into flower.
And, later, the ripening fruit, hanging in the sun,

And the tree, splitting, broken by weight
of pears; and all that pain, all that
erotic crushing in the grass. Remember
all that falling. Then was a time

of wild excitement: us two crossing the sea,
those voyages, the desert in China. Frères humains,
remember the assassinating wind, the withering
of fruit and the last raking of the grass.

And now this place on the parched chasmic alleys,
in the blue streaming rain. "This is our miracle!
said the guide: "our city." Soon, the ulcer will burst –
like a firework! – the unreality destroying itself in light.

This street at midnight marvellously breathing neon
flashes over the brown skull of sinanthropus – glistening
man stretched upon the roadway nailed. O
city of people, Frères humains! Heaving

exhibitions, automatic nodding machines vomiting
truth out of these buildings. City, black mask
at the wedding-feast – a man without a garment?
Only remember the love born of the sniggering games

in the boozing Swan hotel. And then
at golden noon, skyscraper plumes over the city waving
to a child crying in a yard, calling "Come" to his
dad, "Come! Come!" to his Dad.

III ALDERNEY

Eyes left on Alderney island
        lagging behind on a dark island road
strayed where they took them.

Who has stolen my eyes?
In that broken island who could ever find my eyes?
        My eyes are caught

fast in the wire on that hill.
        I should have kept them.
Out of the sea mists descend and

        blind there, bind and kill their
victims in the white cottages
        of roofless Alderney. Now, dark

colony of gulls screams without reason,
    so pain should be as dead as this stone,
that pain as forgotten as stone.

    I stood to watch.
I was Lot's wife in reverse.
Who came stripping, stripping the stone,

wrenching away seaweed, decrusting,
    cutting the black rind from the rock?
I ask. Once, wondering,

Once I uncovered the flesh of the stone:
buried under that growth was nakedly
    cold live unnervingly cold

cold lust. Alderney! *Lustig!* eyes split
    upon Alderney *lustig!* holiday pain
-ful as Fall revealed Alderney, and me.

No War Is An Island.
God, I am Alderney, I am myself,
    I see through estranged eyes

left upon Alderney, lagging behind
    upon a dark island road
with the sea all around, waiting.

IV ELEVEN O'CLOCK

You are the last ones
and the others have passed
        TICK-TOCK
my people and my world being broken up, you
calling, whimpering quietly
        TICK-TOCK
driven into the trampled bones decaying,
from the bread and sweet honey into the wilderness
        MY PEOPLE, and all
into the wet roads and the black streets.

Out of the depths of the decaying tooth I have cried
    MY BRIDE,
COME! O incorruptible timelessness of you
all
    TICK-TOCK
my people!

I saw my people moving strugglingly and dragged on.
Some came leaping
over the crippled, the tortured and intransigent
torturers, and those who were sleeping
and you and I SAW YOU
into the intricacies of perception and premeditation
and questions with too many answers, into the unbelievably soft
arms of them that crept about at noontide
hating, whoring
with corrupting hands
    TICK-TOCK
fingering the nerves laid bare in the decay
    TICK-TOCK
swinging upon the tendons
    TICK-TOCK
mechanically
    TICK-TOCK
    TICK-TOCK

But remembering your are mine, MINE,
I am
my people and I remember
    TICK-TOCK
I never forget green land fried and people laid waste
And you are the last ones,
last ones of all. Until
    TICK-TOCK
Stroke of Midnight.

A Hymn by Damian Lundy

(No date; no music)
Based on 2 Corinthians 1

Refrain

Blest be the God and Father
of Jesus Christ our Lord,
a gentle God of comfort
known in his saving Word.

1. The Son of God proclaimed among us
was never 'Yes" and "No".
In Jesus the Father spoke to us:
the word he spoke was "YES".

2. The promises God made in the past
have been fulfilled in Christ.
In Jesus our God he says "Yes" to us,
accepts us as his own.

3. And that is why we make our Amen
through Jesus Christ our Lord:
in Him we say our "Yes" to God,
accept his saving Word.

4. For we are chosen, sealed by our God,
anointed as his own:
the Spirit poured into our hearts
is God's affirming love.

This hymn is interesting because it deals with a theme which particularly fascinated Damian. In his own account of the foundation and development of Kintbury it is this particular citation from Saint Paul which becomes the theological basis for the creation of the YES Weeks.

A Hymn by Damian Lundy

(No date)

*(Music is available; by Frore Ephraim of the Lion of Juda Community,
St Broladre, France)*
Words: Damian Lundy (using John 20: 22 and adapted from the French)

1.
When Jesus breathed on them, he said, "Receive the Spirit!"
When Jesus breathed on them, he said, "Receive new life!"
O spirit of peace, O spirit of love,
Spirit of new birth and of joy. Holy Spirit of light.

2
May Jesus breathe on us, may he say, "Receive the Spirit."
May Jesus breathe on us, may he say, "Receive new life."
O Spirit of life, to console us you come,
Spirit of wisdom and of faith to inspire ev'ry heart.

3
May he breathe on our world, may he say, "Receive the Spirit."
May he breathe on our world, may he say, "Receive new life."
O Spirit of power, give us words to proclaim,
that we may bring hope to our world as we share the Good News.

A Hymn by Damian Lundy

(No date; no music)

This exquisite poem, certainly among the finest of all Damian's compositions, is discussed in chapter 6. As is mentioned there, such a text calls for an equally inspired piece of music which can do justice to the wonderful word painting and imaginative construction of place which the text evokes.

Annunciation

1.
That quiet girl whose eyes are lowered
Listens intently for a sign.
The only sign's the listening,
The half-closed eyes... "Whose baby? Mine?"

2.
"No, his!" No – his! The holy one
Whose word has found an ear in you!
So listen – and let his power be
The life within your body now.

3
Yield to his love? That power must be
An awesome, penetrating rain.
And in her heart the quiet girl knows
Her Lord, and trembles at the pain;

4.
And in her eye a tear is formed.
Her lips to shape an answer part:
"Your child and mine? Then let it be."
A shadow falls across her heart.

5.
Quietly the messenger retires,
Letting the comfort soothe the fear;
Bows to his Lord within the girl,
Starts at the smile behind the tear.

Printed in the De La Salle Great Britain *Newsletter*, January 1998, was Damian's unpublished hymn, *The Visitation*, sung for the first time at the Memorial Mass in Kensington:

THE VISITATION

1.

I dreamt I saw you walking in a garden
and where you trod the ground was white with snow.
I heard the green grass growing in your footprints
as birdsong welcomed God to earth below.

2.

The snow had melted where you walked upon it
And when you smiled the moming sunlight shone.
I heard the springtime filling all creation,
Drawn just as I was by the child unborn.

3.

Your arms were filled with blossom, white and crimson,
A gift for a pregnant cousin and her child.
You ran to kiss her, trembling at her greeting,
Feeling her baby leap. Her eyes were wild.

4

You left the garden then and walked together,
Talking of children quietly, and of God,
You shared the scent blossom, white and crimson,
And on a barren hillside lightly trod.

5

I dreamt I saw you walking on the hillside,
Walking together, and so long ago.
I followed you and breathed the scent of heaven
And where you trod I saw white flowers grow.

Vowmaking

Candle, burn brighter;
Steady a shaking hand.
Candle, burn brighter, whiter, mightier
Burning than ever pure
Purification-candle burnt before.
Candle, burn brighter,
Sending a smoke-swirl rising.
Symbol-flame of an offering,
Candle, burn brighter still.
Candle, burn brighter than ever burnt the stars above
The stars; and steadier still,
Fire, perpetual fire-sign, mightier flame to fill
A mightier heart for the making,
Here commenced,
Shaking, as it awakes.
Candle, burn brighter,
Still growing whiter –
White is the colour of peace, of pureness.
Candle, burn brighter,
And growing whiter still,
White with a redness-tinge –
Red is the colour of martyrdom, martyrdom of the will.
Candle, burn brighter,
Still growing whiter –
Hot candescence to kill
The wax –
White with the golden tinge
of gold more golden than goldness of plate,
Gold for the treasure-house,
Poor man's treasure-house,
Hidden and new
To fill.
Candle, burn brighter,
Steady a shaking hand.
Burn firm as the firm resolve within –
only a trembling reed without,
Trembling in the wind of sin,
Crying for strength to the source of strength –
Every cry straining,

Ever unwaning,
Ever undrowned in the din
Of other noises,
Rattling hard within.
Candle, burn brighter,
Burn as the flame of love; perpetual
Flame of the firm resolve within;
All reason for candle-light.
Flame for the holocaust,
(Candle-flame, brighter!)
Flame for the purification,
(Hot! Whiter!),
Scouring-flame
of life, to glow
In nakedness, white as snow!
Candle, burn brighter –
Candle-flame hotter –
Years to be burned away!
Candle-flame, lighter – to light new awakenings,
Day-star to herald a waking day;
And the burning vows to pay.
Candle, burn brighter,
Steady a shaking hand and a trembling voice.
Candle, burn brighter, whiter, mightier
Burning than ever purest
Purification-candle burnt;
Then vanish,
Your fire-message
Rather lived than learnt.

Poetry gives an insight into the soul. Those printed here span several years. The last offers a reflection on the implications of professing the vows of religion: chastity, poverty and obedience, growing to the spiritual conclusion that these are "rather lived than learnt". It was Damian's ability to "translate" the written and spoken word into lived experience, and to enable others to do the same. What now follows is probably his final piece of writing, a deeply felt contemplation of his life which was coming to an end. It is poignant, humble, reaching out in hope: Damian's

"Eucharistic postcard" to the Trinity with whom he had related all his life. His personal and warm response to Mary about whom he had written in so many touching songs and poems concludes, not with his death but with his resurrection. Damian had an all embracing vision of the mystery of salvation lived in all its intensity by the Father, Son and Spirit, and into which Mary was invited in a special way. He embraces his whole life, Michael to Damian, for he recognises in Peter's healing meeting with Jesus at the lakeside after the resurrection that Jesus helps us to relive the first meeting we had with him and renews the wonder of that occasion and the total surrender in the love that he calls forth. "You know everything. You *know* I love you." Each of us is invited to renew daily that life giving experience, expressed dramatically in Jesus' words in death: "Father, into your hands I commend my spirit" and "It is achieved!" Surrender is the culmination of a painful process: "Not my will, but yours."

Into Your Hands: Damian's Prayer Reflection

The style of the writing indicates that it is toward the end of his life. It is also written hurriedly on two sides of quarto paper.

> Now is certainly the acceptable time, the only time, God's time, when his salvation will be revealed. So I write to him, Alpha and Omega, my beginning and my end: thank you for the life I have lived. It is your gift – so is tomorrow, as was yesterday. You, my Lord – into your hands I place my spirit, with the Spirit of Jesus, my brother. And with my spirit, take all my memories – any soreness, any bitterness, any lack of love; the jealousies, plans and separations; the passing fancies, the excuses and substitutes – the drinking and the running away; the laziness, the lack of prayer, the time I wouldn't give you – all I wouldn't share of myself with others.
>
> > "The graces I resist, the chances I have missed – Lord, in thy Eucharist take and redeem."
>
> Take my life, Lord, and purify it <u>now</u>: there's still so much emptiness, so much unforgiveness and rancour, so much lack of trust. Take me, Lord, and fill me <u>for</u>

always with the Spirit of Truth – so I can be honest with you, my Judge, NOW; – with the Spirit of Love, so I can think of others – especially now. So much to say thank you for, Lord. So much to praise you for. Let me die praising you, not afraid of you, not afraid of death, but loving and very gentle. It will be a homecoming – I look forward to you, my Father, my Lord Jesus, my Spirit of love and praise.

Thank you for Dad and Mum and Mum and Auntie Mary and Terry and everyone who has shared themselves with me and given me life. I needed them and they loved me, so giving me knowledge of you, my God. Thank you for my vocation - forgive my abuse of it and of all your gifts. Simply enfold me with your blessings in death, as you have done in life, and it will be enough, enough, enough.

> Mary – now and at the hour of my death,
> and my resurrection – be my mother.

> Praise the Lord! Thank you , Lord!
> Into your hands - your child,

> Michael
> Damian
> X